MY LITTLE OUTLIER

A Mother's Faith Journey

Finding a successful path forward
when your child is different

MARIE J. ELLIOT

DISCLAIMERS

While this book attempts to share a mother's journey raising a kid who is not stereotypical, it does not attempt to offer any medical advice of any kind. This is not a substitute for medical advice. Also, each child is different and two children having the same conditions may need completely different approaches. The things that work for one child may or may not work for another child. The outcomes seen may be different for different children. Despite this, the journey of raising these children have a ton of similarities and this is what I will attempt to share in this book. From my own experience on this journey, I hope to help support and instill hope in the parents who are taking and who will be taking similar journeys.

ACKNOWLEDGEMENTS

This book was not written alone. I would like to acknowledge my family and friends who have shared their wisdom, support, and their experiences with me. Hats off to these wonderful parents who have supported their children and believed in them! There are many people who have inspired me and supported me throughout my journey as a parent. Without them, this book wouldn't have been possible.

I want to thank my mom Marie who is and was always my inspiration in everything! I love you, Mom! She was a go-getter and overcomer of all odds! I want to thank my dad Antony who taught me to see the lighter side of life and enjoy life despite everything that goes on. I want to thank both my children Melissa and Melvin who are my best friends and my cheerleaders, who always believe in me. I love you both! You were the ones who even told me about writing a book to share my experience with others. We used to joke about writing our journey as a book even years back.

I want to extend a very special thank you to my leadership coach, Jeanny, for helping me believe that I can do whatever I wanted to do and for her support and motivation to complete my book. I want to thank all my writing buddies, my friends and others who believed in me and supported me. A very special Thank you to my friend Stephanie for validating me and providing her feedback and encouragement along the way. She spent time reading and providing feedback on each one of my chapters as I wrote them. I also want to thank my dear friend Ponni for supporting me through her prayers and encouragement along my journey.

I want to thank my colleague Moawad who was the first one to validate my writing and provided encouragement to finish my book. He was the first person outside of my friends and family to take the time to read my book and validate the idea and provide valuable feedback. I want to thank my close friend's daughter Chellam who took the time to do the first round of edits for my book. I want to thank my bestie's daughter Subi for designing and creating my website for my book.

I very special thank you to all my friends who took the time to answer my questionnaire to share their experiences and wisdom for my book. My sincere thanks to all my friends who read the completed book and shared their feedback. My heartfelt gratitude to all of you and others whom I have not mentioned.

TABLE OF CONTENTS

INTRODUCTION

As we shuttle from hospital to hospital, wondering what lay ahead for my little one, the thought of whether there will be a high school graduation crossed my mind. Will my son even be allowed to graduate as he could not take his final exams? Will attendance be a problem? Will all the checkboxes for graduation be met?? What will happen??

As I sat in the local children's hospital, I wondered what awaited us and if my little one would even live. But, as it turned out, he graduated, and it was the happiest day of my life. He could barely stand, but we made it to graduation! It happened! It was pure joy! That scene lives in my head. It was a moment of "Yes, we did it!" and there are no words to describe that moment. I never thought we would be where we are today.

You may wonder why a simple high school graduation is such a big deal. Everyone graduates. Millions of people do! So, what is she talking about? For those of us who journeyed the path of having a little one who is different or unique (hence the term "outliers"), every milestone encompasses a lot of hard work, faith, trust, and hope! Every little success counts—it's is a huge celebration!

You may wonder why the book is titled *My little Outlier*. The title refers to the unique talents and differences of children who are not stereotypical. Outliers have great potential and are so unique that most social systems/school systems and others don't quite know how to easily cater to these children. The systems are put in place to work for typical children, but they rarely work well for our Outliers.

As a first-generation Asian-American, I know first-hand that being different is not always a great thing. People either brush it off as a non-issue or try to shy away from it, leaving behind troubled individuals who could otherwise have reached their full potential. Deviating from the norms and standards is never looked upon well in our culture. While physical differences may be ok, having a mental or emotional difference or being non-stereotypical in any way is not ok. It scares people, and they either take the approach of ignoring it, or they tend to take the approach of believing that it is not true. Often, acknowledging this will inadvertently expose the same in other family members, which is not ok or acceptable.

People are fearful. Fear is usually caused by a lack of knowledge or understanding of the situation. In most cases, if people understood more, the situation would not be as scary! It takes a lot of understanding, education, and courage to face enormous fears. Of course, there are families who are exceptions and handle these differences well.

Knowledge and understanding can be the beginning of over-coming fear!

As a first-generation Asian-American, I don't exactly fit the perfect, geeky child that people often think of when they stereo-type my culture. I was also quite different and unique. So, it wasn't always easy to fit in. When it comes to being non-stereotypical, this becomes even more difficult. Lack of support and understanding from family, along with lack of understanding of how to support your loved one in such situations, makes it all the harder and scarier. Our first reaction is to shy away or deny the situation. We also have a huge serving of guilt that we put on ourselves, leaving us feeling inadequate as parents and feeling trapped.

As a mother who has lived and is still living this journey, I would like to say that there is hope. There is even success beyond just hope. You only must believe in it, envision it, put a plan in place and pursue it. You can totally empower yourself and your child! It is possible! This book will showcase the various phases that take place through the process of getting to authentic success in this situa-tion—my journey with my child. The journey, albeit challenging, has high rewards that are satisfying to the soul. Like all things in life, faith, hard work, and an intense belief in something are very critical to making the desired outcome happen. Above all, it takes courage to embark on the journey; but keep in mind the ultimate outcome that you want for your child.

The journey has multiple phases, including acceptance, drive, seeking knowledge and support, defining success, putting a plan in place, executing, etc. We will explore each phase in this book. While it is recommended that you read the chapters in order, feel free to skip to specific chapters that interest you. Like every journey in life, setbacks are also part and parcel of this journey. I am hoping to showcase my journey and provide hope and support to other parents. No two journeys are the same, even with the same issues. Wherever you are in this journey, our struggles are common, our goals are common, and we are in it together. It is possible to get your parenting on track! You just must believe it and go for it! YOU CAN DO THIS!

CHAPTER 1

The Taboo

Nobody wants to be different. It scares people when they are different from others who are from similar cultural backgrounds or ethnicities. There is an intense feeling of fear and an urge to defy the difference or to shy away from the difference. Nobody wants to be an Asian-American kid who gets in trouble and who is not a straight-A student. If you live in a suburb in the United States, you know what I am talking about. Asian-Americans are typically successful go-getters with high-paying jobs and executive positions. Even their kids are super go-getters, fitting the stereotypical Asian—straight-A's, studying robotics, playing chess, playing sports, attending weekend language classes, volunteering, competing in math and science competitions, and any competition—you name it. It is very easy to feel inadequate in such a culture. You would be the only outlier in this community. For example, visiting the principal's office, seeing report cards that are not what you want to see, and barely making it through the school year. If that was your kid, you would think, "why is my child different? Am I a failure as a parent? Where am I going wrong?" But that's not the truth.

The truth is simple. Not all Asian kids are the same—no kids are the same. We try to fit square plugs into round holes. Would you treat stomach pain with Ibuprofen? Or would you clip your nails with a hair dryer? It all boils down to putting your child in an environment that doesn't fit or doing things that don't fit your child's temperament and learning styles. We blame ourselves and/or our children and end up feeling discouraged. Honestly, the problem is not with you or your child. It is really with the Education System, environment, working style, and our own thinking and working style. Setting up your child in the right environment and giving the right tools and support is the key to changing this situation of feeling stuck, discouraged, and inadequate as a parent. Think about it!

You just need different tools to handle it. Systems cater to stereotypical kids. If your kids are not stereotypical, they will not address your child's needs. You are familiar with only one parenting style, which you have been parented with and have seen. Your child is in an environment that does not help them perform at their best.

On top of that, we put pressure on ourselves and our children to always do their best performance. It is like rooting for someone who has hurt their leg to run faster in a race— and even win. Your kid is not flawed! You are not a bad parent! However, there is room in the system/parenting styles for handling non-stereotypes. You should know that early on. If you use the wrong strategies, you will create utter destruction. This is what is exactly happening to your talented, highly gifted, bright child and a bright successful parent (you)! And here you are, sticking to your taboo and being afraid of acting, leaving yourself and your child trapped. If you are in the Asian-American community you are sticking to your ideal of the perfect child, who is perfect at everything and the perfect parent. I know I did too when I started this journey.

While I am talking about Asian culture, when I refer to "the cultural taboo," there are several other cultures that are similar. The problems are the same, and the struggles and beliefs are the same. We are all humans, and our pains are similar. For example, what would others think about me? I don't want to be different from others. I want to fit in with the majority! I don't want to be a failure as a parent! I want to do the right thing!

I know you love your child to death and would do anything for them. That is why you are reading this book! You are taking the first step. Having a child who is an outlier is no different than handling a co-worker or a manager who has a different working style. Don't we accept that, and don't we work with that? This is similar. Why would you brush off or not accept a child who is an outlier when you would do anything to keep your job or to grow and prosper in your job. Why wouldn't you do the same for your child whom you love dearly above all things in this world??

3

These are amazing smart children. They just don't fit the stereotypical way of raising and educating children. That's all! Their growth pace is different from their peers. Some of these kids are two to three years behind their stereotypical peers. My own dear son had developmental delays and was at least 2-3 years behind his peers, causing inadequate social skills for his age. While his intellectual skills were high, he had challenges effectively interacting with his peers. He was diagnosed with Asperger's syndrome which is characterized by anxiety, attention and over focusing. While he took time, he did catch up with his peers. Eventually, these children do catch up and reach their full potential— with your unfailing love and support.

The word disability makes people think of obvious disabilities. But that is not the case for the children we are talking about. There are extremely talented children who learn differently and who are being put in environments and situations and systems that do not work for them—making them severely disabled in terms of their functioning. There are so many children capable of highly functioning if they had different support systems or different education systems—they would succeed! The experiences and methods we will discuss can be used both for children who are highly functional as well as those with more challenges. The outcomes may vary depending on the situation but following the methods could create better outcomes and better experiences for both us and our children.

For several of us, it is not our own taboos and beliefs that are roadblocks. There's also a lack of support from family members and friends, and their beliefs make it hard to provide support and care for atypical children.

Summary

1. Being different from others in not bad.

2. No two kids are the same.

3. Educational systems cater to stereotypical kids.

4. Setting up your child in the right environment and giving the right tools and support is the key to success.

CHAPTER 2
Early Signs

In the early days of the journey, it is hard to grasp what is going on. It is typical to feel overwhelmed, confused, and worried. Things are not clear about why your child is behaving a certain way or why your child is throwing tantrums for things that he/she is supposed to do. Many of us don't understand the root cause of the behaviors in the early days of this journey. However, there are several signs that can be used to understand what the behaviors mean. A parent who has experienced this journey would quickly pick up on the cues. In the beginning, I was not clear on why my child reacted a certain way in certain situations or why my child was dawdling.

Here are some early signs based on my own experience that could help you understand what is going on with your outlier:

- Your child takes four hours to do a fifteen-minute homework assignment.

- You usually need to tell your child to do something multiple times.

- Your child deliberately disobeys you.

- Your child cannot pay attention to other information or observe anything else when they are working on a specific task.

- Your child goes to a birthday party, and other kids return happily while your child returns in tears.

- Your child cannot handle any changes in schedules and activities.

- Your child becomes obsessed with one thing for a period and cannot stop playing with it (e.g., cars, drawing, anime).

- Your child has difficulty transitioning between tasks.

- Your child often forgets to do homework and other important tasks.

- Your child dwells on any negatives for long time periods of time.

- Your child has an all-or-nothing attitude (e.g., "I am not good at anything" or "If I fail this algebra test, I suck at math").

- Your child often gets angry when you ask them to do something.

- Your child's teacher calls you for a meeting because your child is causing some problems.

- Your child gets into trouble during recess.

- Your child struggles to get up and get ready for school in the morning

- Your child stays in the bathroom for a very long time when they have something specific to do.

- Your child is prone to meltdowns.

- Your child has difficulty staying on track when they have something to do.

- Your child has difficulty planning and prioritizing.

- Your child blames you for their issues (You will get more of this in their teen years).

When you first notice some of these signs, they cause immense shock, sadness, and a feeling of, "What is going on here?" "What is wrong with my child? These are normal reactions. It is ok to feel sad and shocked initially. It is likely that these experiences are all new to you. You may even wonder if it is your inability to be an effective parent that is causing all these issues. This is usually accompanied by, "Why me? Why is this happening to me? What did I do wrong?" Blaming God, praying, and hoping it will all magically go away one day is also part of the process. When I first noticed these signs, I felt the same and was worried and confused.

There is usually an equal portion of guilt and "What did I do wrong? Am I not a good mother? Am I not a good parent? Did I do something wrong when I was pregnant? Am I a terrible parent? Maybe I missed something important? Maybe I cannot discipline my child properly and set limits, or am I totally overreacting?" You may lean on your dear ones for support, and low and behold, they say you are overreacting! They may even think that it is just a phase, and it will go away—the child is just different, and the child will outgrow it.

After a while, you start to feel physically exhausted, overwhelmed, and barely get through the day. You may feel disappointed in yourself, lose faith, start avoiding friends and others who don't understand your situation, and you may feel ready to give up. Does this sound familiar?

Perhaps you barely get through work and feel less confident and start working harder and longer—possibly to forget your home situation. Ring a bell? You try to pretend that it was nothing, and low and behold, nothing changes. You are back to the same behaviors, the same blowups, and the same issues. You feel terrible and wish you had a magic wand that could make everything alright.

Then you go back to the same guilt cycle. In the early days, these signs and emotions are normal for you and your child. You go through loops thinking if I do this, things will change. If I speak like this, things will change. If I am stricter, things will get better, and my child will do better.

Once you as a parent have pulled yourself together and are really looking at the situation with fresh eyes, we will see what happens next. With an open mind, you can put the clues together and figure out what is going on and what should be done. This is no different from any challenging situation you have faced at work and worked through.

It's time to feel happier, empowered, at peace, and hopeful and understand how your child's behaviors can turn around for the better!

Summary

1. You are not overreacting!

2. There is nothing wrong with your parenting.

3. It is normal to feel overwhelmed when you first notice behaviors and signs.

4. Once you have pulled yourself together, it is time to feel happier, empowered, and hopeful.

CHAPTER 3

Playing Detective

Once you have calmed down a bit, put your logical self in control, and you will be ready to investigate what is really going on with your child. Yes, you are ready to be Sherlock Holmes! It is hard to detect anything without the details. Our memories are often poor when we are upset, hurting, and in crisis mode. So, we need some tools in place to gather the data to play detective. You need a place to go looking for clues, Sherlock!

What worked for me was keeping a daily journal of the incidents (good and bad—what worked and what did not work). I started journaling in 2009 when my child was about eleven years old.

I have been journaling for thirteen years now. The journal served two purposes:

1. It was an outlet for my feelings and observations and a form of venting. I often felt better after I journaled. It was almost like venting to a friend.

2. It was a good record of what led to events and thus served as a source of analysis and supporting information.

Here are some actual sample entries from my journal with personal information masked. You don't have to be too elaborate as you may be exhausted some days and not in the mood to journal— that is perfectly ok. We are not always at our best, and our best varies over time:

10/4/2009: My child had a meltdown when I said we could not go to his favorite store on Saturday. He had a major meltdown. I told him he had five minutes to vent and no more. He was upset that I gave him a time limit. He said, "Who told you to cut me off?" I explained that it was for the good of all. He seemed fine after I gave him a big hug.

10/6/2009: When I came back from work, my child wanted to eat out. I said no. He threw a fit and went into avalanche mode. I was mad and cut him short. Felt bad afterward. But got over it. He was fine.

10/8/2009: I picked up the kids. My child was already upset and was saying he had a bad day. I felt very nervous and said, "Here we go again," to myself. I was frustrated that when I had plans of having a nice evening, it was always ruined. He said he would share after. But I was anxious and asked him to talk about it. It turned out to be some issues that could be fixed. We learned from it and moved on.

10/13/2009: Good day!

10/27/2009: Rough morning – My child lost his ID card. He was so anxious about how to buy lunch and how to use the library without a card. He would not stop. I offered money for lunch and alternate suggestions. He continued to rant. I was so frustrated that I yelled. Then I took him to school. I went to the office, paid for the new ID card, and made sure it was delivered to him during lunchtime. It was tough. Left me tired and frustrated.

These are only a few samples, and there is no rule to the way you need to write in a journal. Here are the topics to pay attention to when you are writing your journal:

1. Behaviors that repeat more often than once.
2. Settings where the behaviors occur.
3. Events leading up to the negative behavior.
4. Players that are involved in the setting.
5. Triggers from people or things that make your child act a certain way.
6. Things that cause anxiety for your child.

After collecting journal entries for a week, I go back to review my entries. At one point, when I went back to read the entries from the past two months and saw what really happened, I made several observations. Obviously, there were some good days and some not-so-good days. There were behaviors and responses that worked and some that did not—it was intriguing. There were clearly different cases, so I continued to journal and review my entries. After a few weeks, I started seeing a pattern emerge. I noticed interesting trends like pure manipulation, disobedience, pockets of child's lack of abilities to handle certain situations (e.g., transitions, surprises, unclear expectations, etc.). The information interested me quite a bit, and I was a bit relieved to know that not everything that happened was due to the child's inabilities. Not everything was due to my lack of parenting skills. So, in a way, it gave me some relief, understanding, and hope that I could handle my child and create better outcomes in daily situations.

I would recommend that you start journaling immediately. It is a great troubleshooting tool and, at later stages, is a measure of progress. Journaling provides insight into how to fine-tune your approach and information about triggers in your child's environment and settings. It is never too late to start journaling! You can start on this journey at any point in your child's life. While it is good to start early, better late than never. You can still create positive outcomes and see results at any stage of your child's life.

While it is recommended to begin journaling in the initial discovery stages, it is a great idea to keep writing throughout the journey and review your entries periodically. You will derive tons of insights from the review. While you are your own detective, there is also merit in getting your child formally evaluated by a professional. In fact, you should get your child evaluated as soon as you suspect something may be "off." The evaluation could reveal more information and/or confirm what you have detected by yourself. It will also serve as formal documentation, which you can use in the later stages when you work on the accommodations for your child. For those who don't have a supportive spouse or family members who supports getting their child evaluated, this could be a challenge, but you will have to work through it.

Summary

1. Detecting the issue needs a journal or log of behaviors and incidents.

2. Journaling should be part of your daily routine.

3. Journals have the data to derive meaningful conclusions and actions.

CHAPTER 4

Evaluations and Medications

Once you have made observations on the behavioral patterns of your child, it may help to get your child evaluated to get more specifics about what exactly is going on. Seeing a good age-appropriate psychiatrist or psychotherapist would help understand and break down the behaviors. There could be several factors that hold you back from getting your child evaluated:

1. The cultural stigma of behavioral evaluation being a bad thing.

2. Worry and fear of the unknown— what will the future hold?

3. Lack of family support.

4. Fear of medication and side effects—what if my child's health is ruined, or what if my child must be on this life long?

5. Fear or shame about what others will think.

While these are normal feelings, you need to take a leap of courage and do it! Is your fear greater than your child's future and well-being? Does the unknown bring more fear than hope? Then it is time to get your child evaluated. Knowledge is power! The more you understand your child's behaviors, the better you can help him/her. Ask around, talk to friends, and research reviews of providers—pick one and go for it! Remember, just avoiding or pushing the problem under the rug does not make it go away but addressing it can make it go away in time! Remember, nobody can force you to do anything without your consent. Nor can they force you to accept any treatment for your child unless you consent. So, just getting your child evaluated does not take rights and control away from you. Treat the evaluation as education and information for you.

Also, note that you don't need an evaluation to begin helping your child. You can start almost immediately by making small changes at home. Start making changes in your parenting style while waiting to get your child evaluated by a professional. Start taking notes and observations that could help the professional.

You can also request an educational evaluation, and if you are unhappy with the progress after the educational evaluation, request an IEE (Independent Educational Evaluation) with a neuropsychologist. You can search for these terms on the internet and there are many resources that will come up. You can also independently take an appointment with an age-appropriate psychologist outside of school. At the time I had my son evaluated, I did not understand what support the school systems had for this and hence went with an independent psychologist outside of school.

A Note on Using Medication

A lot of us are not too keen about using medications of any kind—let alone drugs prescribed for mental health. This is also a cultural taboo. Also, the truth is that most medications have side effects. Though I was not keen on using medications for my son, I did explore the available options. While I was exploring medications for my son, a doctor once told me that the key tipping point is whether the side effects pose a bigger risk to the child's health and well-being than the effects of the condition itself. Keep in mind that not all medications need to be taken forever. There are ways of weaning off them. So, I would just like to say that please do not be afraid or shy away from medication. Explore the options and understand them well (the side effects and the time taken to wean out of them) before you decide. In most cases, behavioral therapy works together with the medications, so your child won't be forced to solely rely on the medications.

Again, we won't go into specifics as this book is not a substitute for medical advice. All I want to say is while there is merit to not exposing your child to these medications, keep an open mind. Medications should not be seen as a way to relieve yourself from your responsibilities to your child. Your support and involvement will make the most difference in your child's life. Medications are not magic.

The truth is that medications can have significant side effects. So, they shouldn't be casually dispensed to your child. The mental health professional knows best, but you as the parent have the discretion of making the final decision about your child's action plan. You need to research and think before you administer any medications to your child. Always keep the bigger picture in mind, as perspective is everything. One dot on a scatter plot is not a good representative of the whole data set. Do your research and background work before you proceed. Nobody can force you to give any medication to your child without your consent. Keep an open mind, learn about the medication, and do all your research before even considering putting your child on it. Also, investigate alternatives that may be viable and equally effective. You should also consider medications that can be easily weaned off and those that have lesser side effects.

Many family counselors and clinical psychologists only recommend prescribing medications when therapy is part of the process. That way, the therapist or psychiatrist can regulate and check in on the patient to see if the medication is working. Ideally getting Cognitive Behavioral Therapy in conjunction with medication is best. Cognitive behavioral therapy (CBT) is a structured, goal-oriented type of talk therapy. Cognitive therapy and family/parental support may be enough in some cases, and medications may not be prescribed. Each child and situation should be explored individually. Again, this book is not a substitute for medical advice. Please consult your child's doctor for specific medical advice.

Summary

1. Overcome your own fears and hesitations.

2. Get your child evaluated.

3. Understand your child's behaviors and treatment options.

4. Understand the proposed medication options.

5. Look for, and lean on viable alternatives, such as cognitive therapy, before trying any medications.

CHAPTER 5

Getting Help and Resources, you can Turn To

O nce you have determined that your outlier needs a stronger and more adaptive support system to thrive, and you decide that you want to be on this journey with your child, the next step is to decide what action needs to be taken. For most of us, this is new and something we have not experienced or seen. Most of us don't have family members we can turn to for advice or don't have examples to turn to for pointers. On the other hand, some of us may already have family members who have gone through this journey and can guide us. Either way, it is good to know where to get help. It's hard to make this journey alone, so extra guidance and support are always beneficial. Each child is unique, and their needs are unique. Each condition is also unique and manifests itself differently in every child. It is important to acknowledge that most people need outside help.

In terms of help, there are several resources you can turn to. There are several books you can get based on your child's situation. I have read many books during my journey. Being a working mom, it was hard to find a lot of time to read. I used to read before I went to sleep. It is hard to keep your eyes open after a long tiring day, let alone keep them open to read small print late at night. Sometimes you can also skim and scan through chapters to get the specific information you are interested in.

Not all books you buy will be useful. Some of them won't have answers to your specific questions. But there are quite a few good books out there. Some of the helpful tips I gained over the years are from books. I learned about preparing my outlier and what to expect before my child experienced any social or classroom situations from one of the books I read. The book that was helpful to me was *Mind-Body Workbook for Anxiety* by Stanley H. Block and Carolyn Bryant Block. The tips in the book showed me how to mitigate the anxiety levels of my child. I also recall a great suggestion from a good friend of mine about how to express what you expect from your child. For example, if I want my child to finish homework by eight pm, I will say, "I enjoy watching Food Network, and I would like to watch it with you after eight pm. Could you finish your homework by eight pm so we can watch it together?" Express to your child what you clearly want. Children want to please their parents, but they don't like being told what to do without any explanation. Treat them like you would an adult. You wouldn't expect someone to do you a favor without explaining why you need them to do it. The same goes for your child. Explain things to them, so they are aware that you want what is best for them.

The idea is to read books to get tips and ideas. Audiobooks and eBooks are great resources as well. I have been enlightened by many TED Talks (short talks on specific topics) and audiobooks I listened to while I was driving back from work or to places.

The second important resource is the Internet. Some of you may think that information on the Internet cannot be trusted 100%. While that can be true, you can still use the Internet to get the lay of the land. Of course, you must take the information in the context it's presented. You should use your own judgment when using the information on the Internet. One of my good friends shared that they found insight or solutions in the chat conversations on several parenting websites.

Connect with parents who share similar experiences as additional resources. It's important to talk with other parents or caregivers who have gone through or are going through similar journeys. I cannot emphasize the importance of this resource. If there are any support groups you can join, take advantage of the groups, and join. Some support groups are virtual. There are even private Facebook groups. These groups provide support and great information.

Opening to your friends, family members, colleagues, and other parents who are supportive of your journey can help as well. Oftentimes, we know the answer, but we just need to talk it out or have someone validate us. Sharing your situation with others can help foster ideas and identify patterns that you were not able to see by yourself. The second advantage is they will connect you with others who are on the same journey or have done similar things. You will be surprised at how connections work and grow. Some of us may not be comfortable sharing such information with others. It is perfectly ok not to go this route. In my experience, when I shared information, it was with a friend of a friend who was on a similar journey. It was helpful to connect with that individual and get the support and resources they were using. I was grateful for the connection.

If you have already gotten your child assessed by a neuropsychologist, use that professional as a source for referrals to schools and other education centers which could help. One of my good friends shared that occupational therapy helped her child integrate motor activities. She also shared that other extracurricular activities like swimming and skating helped with reducing hyperactive behavior and improving social interactions. My friend received this information and referrals from her child's neuropsychologist.

The school district websites and offices could be good resources on how the support programs work. The school websites also will list accommodations and the process for getting them. I received the best information that helped my child through the school guidance counselor. Your child's teachers are also great resources. Having a chat with them will go a long way in getting the help your child needs. One of my good friends shared that after talking to her child's teacher, they put her child in the 504 programs, which helped immensely. Section 504 of the Rehabilitation Act of 1973 (commonly referred to as Section 504) is a federal law designed to protect the rights of individuals with disabilities in programs and activities that receive federal financial assistance. Those programs include public school districts, institutions of higher education, and other state and local education agencies. To qualify under Section 504, a student must have a disability and that disability must limit a major life function. A 504 Plan is a plan developed to ensure that a child who has a disability identified under the law and is attending an elementary or secondary educational institution receives accommodations that will ensure their academic success and access to the learning environment. You can learn more about how to go about setting up a 504 plan for your child from the school counselors. There are many internet resources and websites that provide details on this. You can search for these terms on the internet (i.e., Google them). The 504 plan is less formal and less involved than an Individualized Education Program (IEP). I was not aware of such plans until much later. My son's High School counselor told us about this in his sophomore year. While it was very late in the school stages that I found out about this plan, his 504 plan was a game changer for my son.

The school's special education program can also help. One of my good friends shared that her child had a wonderful IEP case study teacher and many other special education teachers who worked with her child and supported the child's growth. An Individualized Education Plan is called an IEP. This is a plan or program developed to ensure that a child with an identified disability who is attending an elementary or secondary educational institution receives specialized instruction and related services. The IEP process involves educational evaluations, and then the student is classified into different tiers to provide them with the services they need in the least restrictive setting. You can contact your child's school's special education contacts for more information on how to setup an IEP for your child.

Tutors can also help with school coursework. I would also suggest looking into the school's resource specialists and checking to see if there are teachers equipped with the knowledge and skill sets needed to help your child. One of my good friends also shared that attending workshops and conferences (e.g., Pathfinders for Autism) helped her to learn about more resources and accommodations available.

Even with all these resources, no single resource will provide the exact plan your child needs. There is some amount of understanding and modifications needed to suit your child's specific situation. Every disability is unique, and two children with the same condition may also appear very different. You are the only person who knows your child and can come up with the best plan that works for your child. Use all the resources and tailor them for your child. You got this! As challenging and scary as this could be, it is not impossible. It just takes time! You need to persevere, and then success is possible!

Summary

1. Read self-help books and other books on parenting

2. Audiobooks are great for people who want to listen when they are driving or just prefer to listen to books.

3. The Internet and social media support groups provide validation and information.

4. Open to other parents who are your friends, family, and coworkers and—they can share their experiences and insights.

5. Refer to your child's doctors and neuropsychologist (if they have one).

6. School resources, websites, special ed teachers, and resource specialists are all helpful.

7. Learn about the schools' special education program

8. Attend conferences or workshops hosted by organizations specializing in these conditions.

9. There is no exact plan for your child's specific needs - understand the resources and modify the plan to suit your child

CHAPTER 6

Devising a Plan and Advocating for Support

At this point, you should have started journaling to keep track of the events and circumstances leading to your outlier's outbursts and challenging experiences. We will see how to use the journal and determine the areas that are challenging. We will also see how to reach out and advocate to get the support needed by your child and put a plan in place. Once you put a plan into place, you are on your way to achieving the vision you have for your child.

The first step is to determine which steps to tackle first. These are the top areas causing you and your child the most stress, or these are the top areas that prevent your child from using their full potential and abilities. With a lot going on in your life and in your outlier's life, it will be hard to remember and analyze any specific event and find the underlying root cause. That is where your journaling helps. With the daily hustle and bustle and challenges, you won't easily remember the events leading up to and after your outlier's outbursts or episodes. If you have the notes, then you can go back and look to see what patterns emerge and what situations and events cause stress to your child.

Although there will be many such episodes, there will be certain patterns that continuously emerge. You want to tackle the top two to three behaviors. You should also look at them from the perspective of how they prevent your child from reaching their full potential. The goals of the analysis should be to answer the following questions:

1. What are the events leading up to this behavior?

2. What is the underlying root cause?

3. What could have been done better to avoid this negative event in the future?

4. Who are the key players? For example, teammates, classmates, and teachers.

5. What are the environmental stressors?

6. Are there any beliefs your child has that led to the outburst?

7. How do the behaviors of other people affect my child's environment?

8. How does this prevent my child from being successful or performing to their fullest capability?

Once you have answered the questions and identified the top two or three areas you want to tackle, you can start devising a plan that will help negative situations go smoother than they did in the past. For example, if your child threw a big fit and drama over a last-minute change of plans (i.e., running an errand before dropping off the child at a friend's place) because they were not aware of what the task was and became anxious or were caught off guard, your plan would be to talk about the change of plan the day before. This will mentally prepare the child for the day or event. Think through what changes to the schedule, environment, players, and beliefs could have led to a better outcome for your outlier. For example, one of the patterns I found was that my child did not like any change. Any change to what he was expecting would throw him off, causing immense stress, and hence, not being able to be the best he could be. I found "change" to be the root cause of a few outbursts.

Once you find these underlying causes, figure out who you could approach to change the setting to accommodate your child—teachers, counselors, schedulers, principals, other staff, or anyone who has access and authority. Set up appointments and be prepared to talk about specific examples and how the outcome could improve with specific support. It is better to write things out prior to the meeting and rehearse. If your child has an IEP or 504 plan (see section earlier in the book on resources for more information on these terms), you will need documentation to revise the plans. Your child may need additional tests or assessments. No one book can provide a specific set of rules for you to follow. Your child's needs will change with time, and things vary from circumstance to circumstance. I will share some examples of a few of the cases based on my own experience and my friends' experiences. Once you get the parties to agree about how to support your child, ensure the modifications are in place, follow up, observe their progress, and alter things if needed.

Once you execute the plan, you should see significant improvements in the areas you identified. Will it be foolproof 100% of the time? Not at all! The plan will work most of the time and you should have less drama and less stress most of the time. However, there will be times when you are busy with other parts of your life, and you forget to prepare the child ahead of time. As a result, your child will continue to behave in the same way and throw a fit when you forget to prepare them.

For example, you got super busy at work and totally forgot to tell the child that they had to go to after-school care the day before. You had to tell the child right after school. As a result, they were surprised by the change in expectations and have a melt-down. Alternately, you did remember to tell your child that he will have to work on his math homework, but the child still has a tantrum because they forgot or because they are tired. In my experience, the plan will work 80% to 90% of the time. So don't be discouraged if the plan doesn't work every single time.

A plan is a plan, and it is not the absolute rule. Remember, you are human, and so is your child! So don't forget to practice empathy for yourself and your child. This should be the guiding force in all that you do. This is very similar to changing a habit. If you decide that you want to break a habit, like smoking, for example, you won't just magically wake up one morning and never smoke again. You must make an action plan and then stick to it. There will be times when the craving kicks in, and you may cave in, but your support system will hold you accountable. Just like how quitting a bad habit can take time and conscious effort, you need to grant the same mercy to your child. Expect slip-ups but hold them accountable. In that same manner, have your partner or friends hold you accountable for your parenting.

Here are some testimonies of how some parents advocated for their children and the results that they saw:

Quote 1: From Jaylene S, mother to a son on the Autism Spectrum

The impact of our son's medical issues was not being taken seriously. We worked with our neurologist to write a letter to the school and hired an attorney and an advocate to keep him in general education classes for most of his day.

Quote 2: From Jennifer S, mother to a daughter on the Autism Spectrum

When my daughter was in kindergarten, during any school functions, the teacher did not allow my daughter to participate. Her excuse was

only children who can count from one to ten are allowed. But we fought with the school administration, and then she was allowed to sing with her classmates. The teacher and teacher's aide still did not treat her properly. So, we switched to a different school for my daughter. It was like night and day in the new school. She learned a lot and gained confidence and friends in the new school. The teachers were so nice to her and helped her with her numbers and to speak clearly.

Quote 3: From Vandana B, mother to a son on the Autism Spectrum

I chose a school that would be more understanding. The neuropsychologist who assessed my child referred us to the school. The teachers were supportive and gave extra time to complete the written work. Of course, a few children would tease my child, but there was another child who would stand by my child and be protective. I would personally drop in and pick up my child from school. I formed a rapport with all his teachers. They were immensely supportive throughout primary school.

At the secondary level, academics became a challenge again. Though I personally tutored my child, some subjects were overwhelming. The upside is that he began to show a keen sense of rhythm and played the keyboard quite well. So, I shifted him to a less demanding schedule of schooling, and he was able to complete his secondary education. Following that, I felt a course in music would be his forte. He has completed Level 8 practical exams on the keyboard and is pursuing music theory too. He has also shown considerable interest in composing and recording music. I was fortunate to get music teachers who understood him and taught and encouraged him accordingly.

Quote 4: From John D, father to a son on the Autism Spectrum

When our first son was two-and-a-half- years-old, we noticed he wasn't increasing in his vocabulary and he would echo the same words repeatedly, which is called echolalia. We moved from Idaho to Utah, and he began working with a program, Kids on the Move. They sat and observed and played with him and diagnosed that he had PDD, Pervasive Developmental Delay, which was on the Autism Spectrum. We were grateful we could find out early on, so we could get him signed up for an IEP. He went to a specialized preschool and a specialized school for the first, second, and third grades.

Quote 5: From Victoria H, mother to a daughter on the Autism Spectrum

Some teachers in the school would only write the homework on the board daily, and my child would not write it down. I had to do quite a bit of convincing and lobbying to get my child evaluated and get the therapy and medications needed. For homework, I talked to the teacher and said the child would write down the homework from the board, and the teacher would sign off when the child came by to show it.

Quote 6: From Kaylee M, mother to a son on the Autism Spectrum

I had to be in touch with teachers and counselors to help during the school days. During college, I had to be the researcher and act as a liaison between the disability resource center and my child— some of the things were complex and needed translations. In some cases, some of the homework or classwork won't make sense to my child, and my child wouldn't get help from the teacher— I would research and help explain the issues.

Quote 7: From Anand R, father to a son on the Autism Spectrum

At school, I would always meet the teacher in charge and the other teachers who interacted, with him. Once they understood him, it was easier to move forward. They were accommodative and would keep me informed about his progress and lapses.

Quote 8: From Christine J, mother to a daughter on the Autism Spectrum

My child was very introverted and won't say much. When we are in a restaurant, she feels too shy to order from the Menu. We had to speak for her.

Summary

1. Identify the top two to three areas to tackle.

2. Analyze factors causing stress.

3. Think through what changes could make the situation better for the child.

4. Reach out to the people/players who are involved implementing those changes.

5. Suggest and advocate any necessary changes.

6. Document the changes and formalize to them to make it an IEP or 505 plan.

CHAPTER 7

Norming & Performing

Once you have advocated and put a plan in place, share the plan with your child. Remember, outliers don't like surprises. So, it is best to explain things in a way your child understands and can execute. You may have to break down the plan into chunks, write it down, display it, or whatever form is easy for your child to understand, remember and follow. Some kids are visual learners and making posts or visual reminders like drawing pictures or making charts will help. Make your expectations clear and follow your rules diligently. Remember, a clear pattern and routine are needed for your outlier to function. You and your child should hold each other accountable for following the plan.

For example, one of the accommodations that I had worked out with the teacher in elementary school was to have the child copy the homework written on the board and get a signature from the teacher in a small notebook. This was to help my child keep track of the daily homework and when the homework was due. This was also a way for the teacher to help check if the homework was noted down correctly. Another added benefit to this is that writing down the homework helps your child take on the responsibility of completing their tasks.

Once we agreed to this accommodation, I spent time explaining to my child what was expected from him and the teacher. I also got a small, cute-looking notebook and told my child that for each day he executed the plan, he would get a star on his board. Ten stars got him a treat or a small toy. I also explained how this plan will help him do the homework correctly and hence, ensure that nothing is missed or miscommunicated. So, accommodations were explained, expectations set, and motivational reward plans arranged.

Follow up daily to see how your child is doing, and how the plan is working out or helping. Periodic assessment is important. Make a note of what works well and what does not. Don't hesitate to modify the plan as needed. You will see your child's performance improving. Every bit of improvement builds on each other; it is almost exponential. Of course, you will have some downs, but it is important to celebrate every small victory.

Once you have your plan, execute the plan and you should see instant improvements in those areas. Will it be foolproof 100% of the time? Not at all! The plan will work most of the time, and you will have better outcomes, less drama, and less stress for most of the time. There will be times when you are busy with other parts of your life, that you forgot to prepare the child ahead of time, or your child still throws a tantrum or fit even when you have prepared the child.

For example, you had told the child that you would go to the park together, but something came up and you had to go to the store instead and told the child about the change in the last minute. Alternately you prepare your child that he will have to work on his math homework or practice music. However, the child could still have tantrums either because he or she forgot or because the child is too tired. The point is for the plan to work 80-90% of the time, and that is pretty good! So don't be discouraged if you sometimes find the plan does not work. This is expected.

A plan is a plan -> it is not the absolute rule. Remember, you are human, and so is your child! So don't forget to always have empathy for yourself and your child. This should be the single guiding force in all that you do.

Here are some examples of helpful accommodations and rules set up by some parents with the results they saw:

Quote 1: From Vandana B, mother to a son on the Autism Spectrum

Having a counselor hand-pick teachers that were a good fit was very important. Having a safe space to go to by himself and not have to "talk

through" the problem until he was calm and ready. Having him be able to call me directly from school as I could usually get him calmed down and explain the issue to the teachers.

Quote 2: From Christine J, mother to a daughter on the Autism Spectrum

Prayer has been the foundation of her life since her childhood. Her faith in God and Lord Jesus. Singing Bible songs with motions from YouTube was a big help. She attended Sunday School and a Club that helped with memorizing Bible verses and crafts.

Quote 3: From Jaylene S, mother to a son on the Autism Spectrum

Make all essential behavior into habits. Children learn better when they know the ground rules, their boundaries, and what is acceptable and what is not. Do not permit laxity or show preferential treatment. I was firm with my child about his daily schedule, about not lagging. When a favorable behavior is practiced repeatedly, it becomes a habit and part of who you are. I did this with my child, of course, with a lot of help and support from my spouse and family.

Quote 4: Marie J Elliot, mother to a son on the Autism Spectrum

For example, one of the most helpful accommodations was to handpick the teachers (we were blessed to have a wonderful counselor who told us about it). Usually, the computer schedules classes - but there is an accommodation that will let the counselor handle the schedule. Having supportive teachers was very important for my child to be able to navigate the high school years.

***

Summary

1. Bring your child up to speed and on board with the plan.

2. Execute your plan.

3. Follow up daily to see how the plan is working.

4. Modify the plan as needed.

5. Make notes of what is working and what is not.

6. Watch for results!

CHAPTER 8

Visualizing the Future (Vision)

Having a vision for the future is probably the last thing on your mind when you are overwhelmed with journaling, playing detective, identifying the areas that need to change, and putting a plan in place. You are probably lost in your present reality. The future seems scary, and there are so many things in your mind other than having a vision or visualizing the future. There are many reasons why this vision is important. You manifest what you envision, and you work towards that. All parts of your system, mind, body, spirit, and energies will go into creating that which you visualize and want the most. It is like a self-fulfilling prophecy. You prophesize what you want for your child and then work to fulfilling that vision. This is called faith—seeing what you cannot see and believing what you cannot believe. When you are in a state of despair and cannot even see beyond today, it is important to take time to visualize and create a vision of what you want for your child. In the beginning, it will feel weird and even more like a lie or false optimism. But you absolutely must do it.

When you have a few moments for yourself, leave aside all the challenges your outlier is currently having and take a deep breath. Allow yourself to dream and visualize what you want your child's future to look like. Dreams have no limits or boundaries. So go for it! Lay out this amazing future for your child visually. The future does not have to be like a final goal or endpoint. I used to visualize this high school graduation ceremony where I was dressed up, with family clapping and cheering my child when he went up to the podium to get his diploma. I created this vision vividly in my mind, and each day or multiple times a day, and especially in hard moments, I would bring this vision to mind. I believed that this would come true someday. In the beginning, it would feel weird and sometimes seem impossible and even a bit stupid. But the more you visualize this vision, feel it, and want it, it will materialize. You can be very specific or detailed even about little things, like the dress you will be wearing at that specific event

Create a visual of the vision and stick it in your room or in the kitchen and look at the vision every morning— make it a habit and soon this will be etched in your mind. You can also set reminders on your phone to review your vision. Initially, this may be necessary, but after a month or so, checking the vision will become a habit. Habits can begin at any time. For example, when you have bad days, you can practice having ten minutes of alone time, and in those times, you can review the vision—again, this can become a habit if you practice for thirty days or so.

The truth is that there are no impossible dreams. You can pretty much dream anything and visualize your dream in detail. Dream big! This is the single most important step to creating the success you want for your child. This vision or dream can change gradually as you navigate the years of your child's life. But you should always have a vision in your head. Believe it and whole-heartedly want it for your child. When you do this, you will see amazing things begin to happen. You will feel happier, and you will also feel like you have something to work towards and look forward to it. A life without hope will be sad and depressing. When you look to the future and what your children's future holds, a vision gives you peace and joy. As we put our faith and trust in the Divine's hands, He blesses our lives. If you are religious, you can also commit your vision to the Divine and pray about it.

The vision you build will be different depending on your outlier's situation. Each child is different! You also do not need to limit your vision to what you see as your Outlier's abilities today. Remember, your child may be experiencing developmental delays, but they may catch up with their peers, or find their own parallel path. Some children may be higher functioning than others. Some children may be more impacted than others. The vision will be the highest immediate next stage or milestone your heart really wants your child to reach—be bold!

As you reach the first milestone or vision, create the next vision, visualize it, dream it often, and live it! This is an ongoing process. At many points in the visualization, you will have severe doubts and questions about the future. Ignore those negative voices. Leave them be. Continue to hold on to your vision. It is almost like a promise you make to yourself. Claim that promise whole-heartedly. As time goes by, this exercise will come naturally, and you will gain more confidence as a parent. As you see milestones and your visions come true, you get stronger and stronger.

Start dreaming bigger! Visualize bigger things for your Outlier!

I want to share a few examples of the visions I had for my own little outlier. In the beginning, I had this vision of my child's high school graduation. I envisioned every single detail, including the crowd where I would be seated and cheering. I kept claiming and believing in this vision until it became a reality. Then I had my next vision/dream of having my child graduate from college. I kept claiming this vision until it became a reality. Then I had this vision of my child completing graduate school and getting his first job. Once that milestone was reached, I continued to envision my outlier being an independent, confident young adult who is successful in his career. I will continue to envision a wonderful happy family life for my outlier as well. I will never stop dreaming and believing!

As you can see, visions can come true because you and your outlier work towards it every single moment!

***

Summary

1. You create what you envision—be sure to envision that you wish to create

2. You prophesize what you want for your child.

3. Make reading the vision a daily habit.

4. It is ok to dream big.

5. Visualize and believe that the vision will happen and that you will experience that moment someday soon.

6. Your vision is a promise you make to yourself. So, claim that promise wholeheartedly.

7. Once you reach your first milestone/dream, dream again, create the next vision, and keep going!

CHAPTER 9

Celebrating Successes Along the Way

In general, we tend to celebrate something only when it is complete. Take anything, a task, a goal, a trip, a journey, an accomplishment; we celebrate when it is completed or accomplished in the full sense. Oftentimes, in life, some of the goals, tasks, or journeys take a very long time. If we are going to celebrate only when we reach the ultimate finish line, some of us may have to wait a long time to celebrate. The reality is that once we reach one goal or milestone, some of us briefly celebrate and then start worrying about or working towards the next goal. When this happens, it almost feels like you are always chasing something that you can never have. You end up feeling frustrated and even stuck.

As a parent, it is easy to feel like you will never reach your goal. That is why it is so important to celebrate little successes along the way. This philosophy also applies to life in general. The most important thing about life is the journey; there are no final destinations while there maybe intermediate destinations. It is important to pause and celebrate each milestone and each destination, or you will wait a very long time with no celebrations, only anticipation. Not to mention that you will end up feeling like nothing good ever happens in your life. This could lead to sadness and eventually depression, leaving you with little energy or enthusiasm for your next journey.

The reality is there are lots of things to celebrate along the way. Little successes, little changes in behaviors, little joys, and little accomplishments go a long way towards creating the ultimate success you are envisioning. Be your own cheerleader. Celebrate your mindset changes in your perspective on things, including the behavioral changes you have made as well as the changes your child has made. While it may be easier to be your child's cheerleader, some of us are hard on ourselves and forget to be our own cheerleaders. A quote from my good friend is, "Every success, big or small, needs to be celebrated!"

The journey can be rough and tiring. But being your own cheerleader and cheering for every little step and every little success, is important to keep you going. It is like an energy boost that you absolutely need. The same is true for your little outlier too. The journey can be tiring, scary, and rough for your little outlier as well. But they are making the commitment and effort to take this path along with you, and they are making strides—small, medium, or big. So, your outlier deserves a celebration!

The celebration can be anything from telling them, "Good job, you were awesome at the game," or, "I loved how you did at your music practice today!" Just a loving hug, a pat on the back, or an acknowledging smile goes a long way in encouraging your child. Children are very sensitive to their parents' moods and expressions. They sense your joys and sadness as well. According to one of my friends, who is a veteran in this journey, being positive and encouraging around the child is of utmost importance. This can also include a trip to your outlier's favorite restaurant or ice cream spot. I recall my outlier loved a certain flavor of ice cream from Baskin Robbins. We would go there to celebrate our little successes together. At other times, we would walk together and grab a cup of soda while chatting. Sometimes we would go to the park and hang out while my outlier did the monkey bars in the park or took some basketball shots. Sometimes I would buy my child's favorite toy like Pokémon or Yu-Gi-Oh cards as a surprise.

One of my friends shared that she encouraged her child in whatever they excelled at, like music. This showed that she believed in her child and gave her child the motivation and drive to excel in other areas as well. Encouraging them to pursue their passions is a great way to build on top of other successes.

My other good friend shared that she accepted her child the way he was and always encouraged and gave positive feedback. She appreciated her child's progress and treated him when he made good progress.

My other good friend shared that the rewards for success changed with age. She would give her child poker chips for TV time, small toys, or treats. As her child got older, she would reward the child with screen time or financial rewards for a big accomplishment. The goal was always to make the reward as small as possible but sufficient to help the child feel accomplished in overcoming a hurdle that they are encountering.

You may wonder what merits a celebration. Any change or a positive shift in behavior warrants a celebration along with positive outcomes and milestones or reaching goals. Anytime your child shows a willingness or puts in effort into making a change, that warrants a celebration. Change is hard, and it is very hard for your outlier. The change or positive shift also applies to you as a parent and is worth celebrating. Cheer yourself up, go get yourself something, or treat yourself to something you love, even quality time for yourself!

Positive outcomes and reaching goals and milestones are easier to recognize and celebrate. But those take time, and they are not immediate. So, it is important to pay attention and pick out the positive behavior changes and celebrate them on an ongoing basis. Another area worth celebrating is when your child shows ownership and initiative. For example, doing something without being told. Use your judgment to decide what merits a celebration. Celebrations encourage your child to take more ownership and initiative and set your child up for success.

Celebrations kept both of us going. It was also something to look forward to and a motivation for the next celebration and next success. You may also want to write these down in your journal. When you have a next rough moment, reviewing these snippets of successes will cheer you up. I used to write these moments in my journal, along with thanks and praise to the Almighty!

Celebration, along with gratitude, gives you a sense of peace and joy. So, make sure you add gratitude when you celebrate the little successes along the way. It also emphasizes that The Divine was with you and is making way for great things ahead and will make your vision come true!

Summary

1. Seeing success along the way.
2. Cheering you and your child.
3. Celebrating successes, big or small.
4. What merits a celebration?
5. Celebrations keep us going.

CHAPTER 10

Preventing burnout and thriving/being flexible

Today's world is fast-paced, and people have busy schedules. It is easy to get burned out and exhausted. If you have the additional task of helping your child who has different needs, then your schedule probably is more packed than others. Having a full-time job and being the sole moral and emotional support for your children, can cause daily exhaustion.

Burnout is inevitable! You may reach a point of burnout, causing depression, health issues, and other problems. It is extremely important to prevent such burnout as you will not be able to be there for your outlier as much as you want to be. Your exhausted body and mind cannot take it anymore. You most likely will second guess your choices and commitment to helping your child thrive.

The key to preventing burnout is to schedule self-care and other activities that give you joy. While it is hard to carve time for yourself amidst your busy schedule, it is possible. It takes conscious effort and prioritization. Making yourself a priority is a must! My mom always taught me how important self-care was when I was growing up. She used a native proverb which meant that you cannot draw a beautiful picture without a good canvas. The proverb meant that if you don't take care of yourself, you cannot do the things you want to accomplish.

Self-care at the core means taking care of your mind, body, and spirit. Nurturing your mind, body, and spirit is vital. For example, nurturing your body includes eating healthy, exercising, and sleeping well. Nurturing your mind involves surrounding yourself with positive thoughts and positive people, reading books, and watching positive and inspiring shows and movies. Nurturing your spirit/soul involves connecting with the Divine. If you are religious, connect with your innermost self, which is God, by reading scriptures, and listening to religious music.

The next question you may have will be how in the world am I going to do all of this with everything on my plate? I must do the household chores and groceries, follow up with bills, sit with my outlier for his homework, drop and pick up my other child, etc. That's where flexibility and creativity come into play. Once you make a commitment to self-care, you will find a way with some creativity and flexibility.

The word flexibility is key here! We all know that when you have kids who are different and need more support and care, things change almost suddenly. A perfect day could be ruined in minutes. A calm morning could become chaotic. A day you planned as peaceful turns out to be one filled with anxiety and turmoil. You may end up having new tasks on your to-do list which were not there before. So, your schedule goes for a toss. Obviously, self-care tasks get pushed down the list and may not happen. You will be surprised what you can fit in if you are flexible and creative. There are many ways to skin the cat, as the saying goes.

Let's say you had planned for a fifty-minute walk, but things didn't go as planned. You can try to fit in two twenty-minute walks in between tasks or just do one fifteen-minute walk. Doing nothing because your plans to go on a fifty-minute walk can't happen will make you feel bad. But if you go for a fifteen-minute walk at least, you will feel a lot better, and your head will be cleared. You can also incorporate listening to spiritual music when you walk. Just let the music clear your head or even tune in to the outdoors. Alternatively, you can do a fifteen-minute run on the treadmill.

Another example is if you planned to make a healthy meal but did not have time, you can always put together a healthy meal by even eating some raw vegetables with dip along with some frozen entries you warm up (I always keep a bunch of stuff handy in the fridge and freezer for such times). You can also talk to your friends during a walk. Being creative and doing some multi-tasking can help you incorporate self-care into your routine, which may not be predictable.

There is also another way you can make sure you get yourself self-care. Incorporate most of it as early as possible before other people in your household are awake. If you are not a morning person, this will not work for you. I was not a morning person, and most days, I couldn't do this. However, I used to read for fifteen minutes in bed before I went to sleep. It was a way to nurture myself. I also loved connecting with friends and family and would do a quick call while I was waiting to pick up my outlier. Basically, it is about being open to different ways of accomplishing the outcome of self-care.

Alone time is another important concept. It means having some time to yourself each day. This is ME TIME! You get to do things for yourself or just sit down by yourself to clear your head. This is a vital part of thriving—it was for me. I usually get this time at work before leaving the office. I would wrap up work, sit down for around twenty to thirty minutes, drink a cup of tea and just be alone, clearing my head. I would let the thoughts be and sometimes do some self-talk. Sometimes, I would just sit there and do nothing. It helped me relax. When I drove back from work, I would mentally run down the things I would have to do when I got home. This prepared me for when I reached home. I could execute quickly and have time to sit with my outlier, help with homework, read books, talk, and even play a small game or have casual chats. You can also have alone times after dropping your outlier for any activity such as sports, etc. I dropped off my kids for their Faith Formation class, then sat in the car or walked around in the nearby areas, clearing my head, listening to music, praying, or calling a friend. You may ask, is this all self-care? Of course, it is!

One of my good friends shared that she would frequently talk to her parents, who allowed her to vent or express herself. Sometimes just sharing your fears, worries, and anxieties with someone who cares for you and whom you trust can be very therapeutic and comforting. We, as humans, need that comfort and knowing that someone listens to us and understands us. One of my other friends shared that sometimes she would just sit in the closet by herself and cry, and that was a healthy thing for her to do. It released her from her anxiety, stress, and tension. She shared that her busy job kept her distracted and kept her going.

Other friends have shared that they would just pray by themselves, venting to God and that helped them feel better. Another one of my friends just took alone time by sitting in the car alone. For parents with children that cannot be dropped off at activities, they can try the morning time when kids are still asleep or nighttime after kids go to sleep. Some parents also have spouses who travel for long periods of time. Hiring a babysitter or soliciting a friend to take care of your kids for a few hours would be options.

Dropping your kids at a friend's place or on a playdate would be another option.

My other dear friend shared that she would read a lot of self-improvement books and listen to devotional songs. Another shared that she would read books while waiting for her child. Sometimes she reads fiction and sometimes self-help books. She also loved places where she could go for a walk or spend time amidst nature which was therapeutic and relaxing for her. Moving among plants and trees helped her drain her negative energy. There is something calming about nature!

So, there are several different ways to take care of yourself, re-energize and get back on your journey. It is very important to remember self-care during this journey.

Summary

1. Be creative with self-care.

2. Schedule self-care—make time for it.

3. Be flexible.

4. Don't forget alone time.

5. Connect with friends and family who are encouraging and supportive of your self-care.

CHAPTER 11

Being Different from Other Parents

As a mother who is committed to her outlier and making her vision her outlier come to reality, you will be totally different from other parents with neurotypical kids. For example, your schedule and your approach to parenting will be totally different. Oftentimes, you will encounter situations where others think you are a helicopter parent who does not want to let go of her kids or who does not know how to let go of her kids. This will often hurt you and make you second guess if you are really doing the right thing. If you are feeling this way, you are not alone. This is common and normal.

Your outlier will continue to need your support beyond the high school years, leading into college and beyond. Most parents will start to or completely let go of their kids once they go to college. When they see you supporting and handholding your outlier, they will think you are weird or a parent wanting control—a helicopter parent who refuses to let go and who does not know how to let go. I have had my close friends, and even my best friend and family members tell me that I need to let go and not coddle my child as much. They have told me that I need to let my child fail and suffer so he learns to handle things in life by himself.

While this is not entirely incorrect and even true, to some extent, context is everything. Remember, the people who criticize you do not know your child. They may have minimal knowledge about what it takes to parent or support a kid who is different. So, it's very important not to take this to heart. At the end of the day, what you want to do to support your outlier is more important than what anybody else thinks or says.

Even if it is your close friends or close family, keep the criticism in context. I have had my best friend, who has my best interests at heart, tell me that I need to step away from my outlier. My friend was coming from a place of love. It worried her to see me tired and stressed out so much of the time. However, what she said hurt and made me wonder if I was indeed doing the right thing. I began to second guess myself. This kind of confusion is normal, especially if you hear it from your close friends or family. People talk from a place of familiarity and from what they know.

In my opinion, it is rare that someone will try to understand things from your perspective or see it from your point of view. But, if you have friends who have children who are different or have challenges, they will understand you. They have similar perspectives and experiences, and they will be able to validate and support what you are doing. At the end of the day, ask yourself what outcome you want for your outlier and if you really want it. This will give you clarity that what you are doing is the right thing! It is ok that other parents/friends don't think the same way. It is ok that you are different!

Something else that could happen is that your friends think you are so busy over-parenting your child that you don't have time for them or any fun. This may hurt you. It will also make you think you are weird or over-obsessed with your child. Your life is so busy and overloaded, and you barely have time to do fun things you like. Hearing these comments will make you feel worse. But wait a minute! Who are these people judging you? Do they really know what they are talking about? Do they have the slightest idea what you are going through? No, they don't.

Family is yet another story. They may think they are the parenting gurus and have a ton of advice for you. For example, they may say you have control issues—you can't let go of your child, you want to keep mothering the child, you are treating the child like a baby...blah, blah, blah!—you are not empowering your child, you are going to cause the child more damage than help the child, when are you going to let go of your child and let them be independent?

I have had family visits where they tell me subtly and sometimes, even explicitly, that my outlier needs to be left alone to grow up and become independent and that I need to back off. They even said that I may have problems and control issues. I had a family member tell me that I am ruining my outlier by not empowering him. All these comments have made me sad and question myself. *Hello family, do you think I have not tried this? Family, do you think I enjoy being a control freak and getting all overworked?* You can provide some appropriate comments to not waste energy arguing with these people like, "Thank you so much for your concern. Thank you, I hadn't thought of that. Thank you, I will give it some thought".

Coworkers are no different from family and friends. They will give you their share of parenting advice based on what they know and have experienced. I have had some coworkers tell me that I am over-parenting. Yeah right! Like they know what they are talking about! I also had a few coworkers who totally got me. They were in similar situations; they understood what I was doing and advocating, and, in fact, they considered me a role model. A colleague who is a good friend has a child who is an outlier. The coworker listened to what others thought she should do. Today, the child is still struggling well into the adult years. The coworker regrets not having been there for the child in the younger years, and now she is appreciative of my perspective. We talked quite a bit and shared our struggles. The coworker is a great supporter of my work. I am grateful to the coworker for all the support and validation. In fact, my coworker was my motivation to write this book. My coworker often says that she wished she could have done the same for her child.

The truth is there is support! You need to enlist support from people who have similar experiences. They know what it takes. They understand the struggles. So, it is best to not to take what your friends and family, who don't know anything about what you are going through, tell you to do. What others aren't seeing is that parts of your child's development are on a much longer timeline. Things their child could do or process at age ten, our outliers are still trying to learn at age twenty. Would people think you are over-parenting if your child was four instead of eight, or ten instead of twenty? Of course not! A very good friend of mine shared, "Having kids who are big for their age makes it worse. My son has been in the ninety-eighth height percentile his whole life. People thought he was sixteen when he was twelve and couldn't understand when he acted like he was six dealing with emotionally challenging situations."

We must fill the gaps in instructions or spell out the implied details in real-world situations for our outliers. We must act as translators between the world and our outliers, and it works in both directions. Another quote from my good friend, "My son was taking a math test today and wasn't sure what format the answer had to be in as it was a free-form answer. He asked the teacher, and she didn't understand his question. I had to interpret it for him, but he was really upset and frustrated. If I hadn't been there to help him, he probably would not have been able to finish the test."

You are a smart person. You know what you are doing, and you totally understand your actions. Of all people in this world, you want your outlier to be independent, empowered, and successful! Trust your judgment; you know when to let go. You are doing an amazing job! It is ok to be different from other parents. You are a great parent! You know what is best for your child, and you are doing all you can for them. So, you will let go of your Outlier over time. It does not have to be on someone else's timeframe. You will do it in the time that works for you and your outlier. But you will eventually get there. So be proud and give yourself a big pat on your back for being an amazing parent! You got this! I understand you. You don't have to be like others, or you don't have to change your commitment to your outlier because other parents think you are different or weird!

Doing what is right for your outlier should be your priority! What others think is their opinion, not yours. So, in summary, you are a great parent! Surround yourself with people who will understand and support you. That does not mean you should leave your friends who don't understand this aspect of your life. You just don't have to talk to them about your parenting. You can still have fun and be with your friends. Just don't expect them to understand your parenting struggles.

***

Summary

1. It is ok to be different from other parents.

2. You will always have many people who don't understand and get you.

3. Enlist support from people who have similar experiences.

4. Doing what is right for your outlier should be your priority.

5. What others think is their problem, not yours!

CHAPTER 12

Progress Check and Revising the Plan

You worked hard to identify what kind of support your child needs and put the plan in place. The plan has started producing results, your child is having some success in school, and things are going smoothly most of the time. I say most of the time because we all know that "most of the time" is good progress. Of course, there will be moments of challenges, which is also expected in this journey. Expecting the same plan to continue to work is unrealistic as things change over time.

Your outlier keeps growing and their environment keeps changing. So, what worked smoothly before may now not work as well, or what was challenging before may no longer be a challenge. That is why it is important to periodically have conversations with your child and assess the situation holistically. Often this re-evaluation will warrant a change in the support plan you have for your child. You should make checking in and looking at what works and what does not work a part of your journey.

You will need to check in periodically throughout your journey as a parent or caregiver for your outlier. This will ensure that your outlier has the right support and right processes in place at each stage of their life. For example, in elementary school, being in touch with the teacher and periodically having meetings and touching base may help your child have better classroom support. While this sometimes works, there are other challenges in the playground or in extra-curricular activities that may arise. You may be thinking everything is going well while, in truth, it may not be. That is why it is important to check in with your child periodically. Periodically may be daily or weekly. Checking in can be a simple "How was your day? How are things going with your classmates? How did recess go today? Whom did you play with? Did you have fun?" Checking in can also be taking your child for a walk, to a local ice cream shop, or to the park to shoot hoops or any of their favorite activities.

Children are more likely to open when you least expect them to. It is best not to put too much pressure on them or explicitly check in and ask for information or feedback. It is best to check in casually and with less pressure. When you check in, you will stumble upon things going well where no change is required, or alternatively, you may find that there are areas that need intervention and additional support. For example, you may find that your child is having some difficulty during lunchtime or recess. So, it is time to talk to the teacher or another staff person who supervises the children during recess or lunch to request support for your child.

You may also want to check in with the staff in charge, such as coaches, teachers, and others who interact with your child. Our children act different in various situations and when they are around adults who operate on different filters/assumptions. Having external feedback is important because it can highlight bad assumptions, areas needing support, or even help us see new areas of progress to celebrate.

Sometimes you may find out that your child is having new challenges in a specific class that went well before. Or you may find out that a new project or teaching style is giving your child a challenge. This is when you realize that the support plan needs to be revised. The plan revision may happen two to three times per year. If your goal is for your child to get better and become neurotypical, that will end badly for everyone. Thinking of new challenges as growth instead of failures is a way to build on the past and move towards the vision you have for your child.

You may also have periods when things are working fine for months, and then you must intervene and change things around multiple times— even within one month. Like always, the key to this journey is flexibility. This is the most important quality that will get you through this journey and create the success you want or envision for your outlier. I can't emphasize this point enough.

You should periodically evaluate the accommodations you have for your child either on their 504 or IEP plan to see if those are relevant and are working well. Just having a plan in place does not guarantee that it is adequate and will also be working or even relevant. Things change in your child's environment. Your child is also constantly growing and evolving. What's needed as an accommodation before may not need be needed anymore. Or an accommodation that worked before may not be adequate.

For example, suppose you had 1.5x (extra time for tests). This time may not work as your child progresses to more challenging upper-division classes— or in college, this time needs to be made 2x (twice as much time) for some of the higher-difficulty technical subjects. Suppose you did not have notetaking as an accommodation. In that case, you might need to ask for it again for certain subjects or certain classes where the teacher is fast-paced or less organized. You may want to ask for additional help when it makes sense. So, don't be afraid to revise the plan for your child at any point. I had to periodically review and adjust my child's accommodations. It is normal, and it is a necessary part of this journey.

Identifying progress or challenges can also be tricky. You may often wonder if your child is really making progress. Sometimes it will take two steps forward and three steps back for your outlier. This may leave you confused as to whether we are making progress or did we regress. Don't worry if you feel this! This is totally common. The important thing to remember is that your outlier will never go back to where he or she started. That will never happen! I know it will be hard to understand this, but trust me, it's true.

When you have situations of regressing, use the eighty-twenty rule. If your child has been on track and progressing 80% of the time, then your child is progressing. Also, if you see the frequency of meltdowns, tantrums, and anxiety attacks reducing, then your child is progressing. Also, there may be one-off incidents, which may not warrant a plan change or plan revision. So, the frequency of the challenging situations and the likelihood of them happening again should be your guide in what to address.

Remember, you are pressed for time and energy, and you need to put your energy and effort toward things that really matter and that will help your outlier the most. You don't want to be chasing things that are a one-off, and things that are not part of the bigger picture. Some challenges and issues may just need a hearty chat with your outlier and won't warrant any changes to the plan.

Some situations or challenges will warrant a much bigger change to your outlier's support plan and life. However scary and big these are, you must address them. Remember, fear is not something you fear! Otherwise, you won't be the parent who is willing to make this journey. Since you already made a choice to go along this journey with your child to see your child successful, pushing forward is how you will overcome your fear. You can take bold steps and march with your outlier through any kind of challenge.

I recall some of my friends had to make the tough choice of changing high schools for their children. Some of them had to move their children to high schools that were an hour's drive each way. They did this because the new school had a better support system and had the teachers and staff to help their children succeed. In fact, I had to do this for my outlier, too, after the first year of high school. It was the toughest decision I had to make, but it was the best decision. I didn't know it at that time, but I can tell for sure now that it was a game-changer!

Changing schools is huge and can have a big impact on your child's siblings, your life, and your child's life. Sometimes the changes are not supported by your spouse, and it may create challenges if you have other children who must be dropped off at another school in another part of town. But none of these challenges should stop you from doing what is right for your outlier and creating the environment and support systems that are right for your child to reach their full potential. It is very important for your child to be in an environment that will set them up for success.

You could spend a ton of wasted energy in situations that don't support your child. There is no one-size-fits-all. You must figure out what works for your child's specific needs. Being afraid of making changes will only make things worse for you and your child, causing daily agony and stress. So, it is ok to make such drastic environmental changes if it is the right thing for your child. Many of my friends have made these changes, and it helped their children succeed and go far. So go for it! It is totally worth it! Remember, ultimately, you want to create that vision you have for your child, and nothing will stop you from doing exactly that! Keep the conversations going! Remember, authentic success does not come free! You work to create that success.

Summary

1. Periodic progress checks are needed.

2. Check-in with your child regularly.

3. Solicit external feedback.

4. Periodically, evaluate the accommodations you have for your child.

5. Environmental settings, players, and challenges may change over time.

6. Identify what to tackle.

7. Go for it!

CHAPTER 13

Seeing Success

You have been working so hard all along to figure out your child's challenges and set up your child in the right environment and put a plan in place that will help your child be successful. This is all hard work, and it takes a lot of energy, time, and effort. This phase may seem long drawn and tiring, but eventually, you will see success for your child, and you will see your hard work and the plans you put in place paying off. While the journey seems long and hard, success is certain!

When you put your body, mind and spirit, and soul into this journey, you will reach a point of seeing and feeling success. Each child is different, and each situation is different. So, there is no fixed time when you start seeing success. Don't be discouraged if your child is not showing progress at the same rate as another child in a similar situation. The key is to commit to the journey wholeheartedly and work through the details. As you do progress checks and rework plans as needed, success will come, but most likely in the time you least expect. The next question may be how do we define success, or what does success really look like in this journey?

Success is defined as "the accomplishment of an aim or purpose." This leads to a question about the aim or purpose of this journey. The aim or purpose could be different for different people and depends on the condition of the child and the specific situations. Mostly, the aim or purpose of this journey is to provide your child the needed environment, tools, and support systems with which they can adapt to their environment, perform, be their best, and reach their highest possible potential.

I always recall what my neighbor said to me several years ago. She is a mother of three children. She said that we should always encourage our kids to be the best **they** can be and reach **their** fullest potential. Prior to this, I thought success was reaching the highest possible place. This perspective has always helped me see success in my children in their own unique ways. Each child is different and has different challenges. One child may have more academic or focus challenges, while another child may have more social challenges. Or one child may be good at reading and writing and have challenges in math, while another child may be good at math but has challenges in reading and writing. One child may be more creative, and another may be more of a sports person.

Your aim or purpose as a parent is to help your child reach their fullest potential. Your aim or purpose is not to make your child reach someone else's potential. This perspective is very important as it can make or break your child. This applies to any child, neurotypical or otherwise.

Success has many forms. When you see your child thrive, it is an indication of success. When you see your child adapt and handle their environment, that is a success. When you see your child overcome their challenge quicker than before, that is a success! When you see your child more confident than before, that is a success! There are measurable and immeasurable accomplishments too. Some of them are harder and more visible. For example, getting good grades, passing a class, and reaching a milestone in a sport or in a classroom setting, are harder and more visible. While having a faster turnaround time from a tantrum or a panic attack or an anxiety episode or being more comfortable in a social situation where your child was previously uncomfortable are all signs of success. These are some examples of success that are subtle and less visible. Any progress is a success! As discussed in chapter 12, celebrating successes along the way is very important. While we are waiting for the other shoe to drop, or the next tantrum, or the next challenge, we should still take time to celebrate intermediate success.

Success in this journey does not mean that your outlier has reached what his other neurotypical peers have reached. Also, success in this journey does not mean you and your outlier no longer have any challenges—although some of us would like to reach that point. Success is not a cure or a state of having no issues. Success is when your child can adapt to challenging situations. Success is when your child can use the tools provided to handle situations more consistently. Success is when your child can effectively and more consistently use the tools they have been taught and the support system they have in place to handle their situations or problems effectively. This is when you can say that you are seeing success with your plans. When you have the right perspective about what success means for your child, you will be able to feel and see success for you and your outlier.

Even when you see success with your child, setbacks are common. So don't be discouraged. When you see a stretch of success and good times, you may suddenly see some of the old behaviors and challenges show up. This may discourage you and cause you to worry. But know that setbacks are very common, and they happen in this journey. The important thing to remember is that you and your outlier will never go back to where you started. Setbacks will come and go. Always use the eighty-twenty rule to measure success. If your child can handle the challenges and use the tools effectively 80% of the time, then your child has reached success.

Another measure of success is the frequency of the times between setbacks. Yet another measure is the time it takes to rebound from setbacks. For me, this has been a very important measure of success. While the child shows some regression back to past behaviors, when you see them rebound quicker than before, that is a success, and you are making progress. It is important to encourage your child and reassure them that it is not their fault and setbacks are common, and they are doing a great job. If a setback is due to the child's lack of effort or any misunderstanding, you can share that with your child and encourage them to turn things around and keep going.

One of my good friends said that she would take it one day at a time, keep loving her child, and not be disappointed with the setbacks. Instead, she would put effort into spending more time with her child, encouraging her child, and continuing to be a big part of her child's life.

My other good friend shared that she would explain to her child that everyone has days that are better than others and that the goal is to keep trying. She also shared that she has not seen a linear progression in her journey but rather a stairway—sometimes two steps back and one step forward. If there is progress occurring in some form, then that is a success for her.

Success was possible through the combined efforts of you and your child and your willingness to work through all the challenges together. Take time to reinforce these successes with your child. Take time to make your child feel it is their success and celebrate each victory. You can do that with and without rewards. Tell them how proud you are and how far your child has come! Help them feel their success—it's their success. Positive reinforcement goes a long way in encouraging your child to continue those behaviors that are working.

Summary

1. Seeing success is certain.

2. It is important to define what success is for each child.

3. Success has many forms.

4. Setbacks are common.

5. Reinforce small successes to see bigger successes.

CHAPTER 14

Teaching to Advocate and Letting Go at Different Stages

In the initial days of your journey, you yourself were learning to advocate for your child. As the journey progresses, you have learned how to advocate for your child in different situations. You understand when you need to advocate and what you need to request. You slowly become a pro at this, whether it means emailing a teacher, asking for a meeting with a teacher, or asking for help for your outlier with instructional modifications or extra support, or other help with organization and homework—or any help at all.

You will always be the main advocate for your child or the master advocate for your child. You know how to act as a translator and advocate between your outlier and the outside world and between the outside world and your outlier. You also know how to recognize situations that warrant advocacy and support. But as your child grows older, it is time to start grooming your outlier as a self-advocate. Teaching self-advocacy will go a long way into their college and adult years.

When your outlier grows older and goes into high school, there will be pushback from teachers and other people to have your outlier talk to them without you. Sometimes, even in middle school, there is a push back from teachers and other staff. In college, of course, your outlier will only be allowed to advocate for themself. So, it is good to start early by teaching your outlier how to self-advocate for themself. This skill will be well useful into the adult years and even in the job life of your outlier.

First, you may start off by helping your outlier understand why they are different and how the school and other systems are better designed to support neurotypical people. This may be hard for your outlier to understand when they are young. Your outlier may even have a hard time understanding why he is different and may misinterpret the difference as a problem. So, it is important to take time and slowly help your outlier understand that they do not have a problem and it is not their fault they are not neurotypical. Then, explain why your outlier needs a different kind of support system to help them succeed.

You can quote examples from the past. For example, remember how we asked the teacher to sign off on your daily homework and how that removed ambiguity in your understanding of your tasks? Remember how it helped you remember what you had to do so you wouldn't miss anything? You can quote more examples of how a change in the process or additional support systems helped your outlier overcome challenges and succeed in the past.

Explain to your outlier that identifying areas where you need help and asking for that help is all part of self-advocacy. So far, as their parent, you have managed all the advocacy. You can tell your outlier that you will continue to be the lead supporter and advocate, but you would like them to learn how to advocate for themself as they grow older. There may be some level of anxiety creeping up in your child as you have this conversation. So, it is ok to slow down and take whatever time is needed. This conversation should not be rushed, and you should not push your outlier into self-advocacy. There is a good chance it will backfire and cause undesired outcomes. So, take time to do this slowly. Once you have established the need for self-advocacy, you can begin to teach your child how to self-advocate.

Here are the steps:

Step 1 - Awareness of the situation - Help your outlier identify areas where they are having difficulty. For example, attending a class with a teacher who is disorganized, attending a class where the teacher does not communicate clear expectations on homework and assignments, and subsequently, having difficulty remembering to turn in assignments, having difficulty with test taking (not enough time), having anxiety when too many things are due at the same time, etc. This first and most important step in self-advocacy is to determine and acknowledge that there is a situation that is presenting a challenge.

Step 2 - What is needed to help with the situation - Help your outlier come up with solutions that would have helped them overcome the difficulty. Examples would be to request a written expectation on homework or assignment that is not clear with oral instructions. Another example would be to ask for extra time for an assignment—if needed. Help your outlier identify what they need to be successful in those specific situations.

Step 3 - Identifying who to ask for help - Teaching your outlier about the school or college system and who to approach for help and which department offers help. You can help research this and coach your outlier who should be approached for help in different situations in high school, or college. In high school it may be a counselor, and in college, it may be the Disability Resource Center. This may not be as easy for your young outlier. It is ok for you to do the research and help them more in this area.

Step 4 - Asking for help - Teaching your Outlier how to set up an appointment, prepare and present their case when they need help. This may include having a meeting with a teacher and explaining the problem/difficulty your outlier is having in a particular situation and asking for modifications or assistance. You can optionally be present in the meetings with your outlier while letting your outlier do the talking. You can augment or add as needed, depending on how the conversation goes. You can also help prepare the documentation or justification needed to get the help. This may sometimes be beyond what your outlier can do. Alternatively, you can prepare your outlier before the meeting, even do some role-playing, and run through "what if" scenarios.

Your outlier may or may not want to do any of these steps for a while, and that is ok. Remember, you are and still will be your child's primary advocate for a long time. But it is important to keep teaching and preparing them for self-advocacy. Depending on the level of functioning, some children may not be able to do self-advocacy at all. This is totally fine. For those outliers who have grown and are able to self-advocate, you assume the supervisory role. You will help talk through ideas, brainstorm new ideas, and find creative ways to get help with your outlier while hearing and encouraging their ideas. You can give input and pointers or even lead some areas of advocacy that are more involved and are hard for your outlier. Your role will be more of a guide or a coach as the years go by, and your outlier grows.

Your supervisory role may also involve auditing or catching improper use of the accommodations provided. For example, your outlier may overuse the extra time on assignments and try to postpone many deadlines, causing lots of stress and anxiety, especially when there are too many postponed deadlines close to each other. As a supervisor for your child's self-advocacy, it is ok to ask your outlier questions on whether that situation really warrants an extension. Also, you should explain to your outlier why misuse of the accommodation may cause more problems.

When your outlier is younger and in high school, this is likely to happen as your outlier sees this as an opportunity to postpone things. Therefore, improper self-advocacy could lead to more problems and stress for your outlier. So, your Outlier should be taught early about how to use their accommodations wisely.

Your outlier won't turn into a perfect self-advocate overnight. You must find the balance between interfering, overseeing, and letting go. There is no way to know how much interfering and how much letting go is right. This will depend on your child, the situation, and the maturity of your outlier. But, as you play around with this, you will get to know the right balance. Will you always get it right? No! It's trial and error. This is part of this journey. Just being open and flexible, like in other aspects of the journey, is key. Eventually, at some point in your outlier's life, you will let them make their decisions and learn to let go. There is no right age for this. You just must stay flexible and positive and keep on with the journey! Good luck teaching self-advocacy! Here is a tip from another parent who is going through this journey:

I signed my child up for a self-advocacy workshop and had self-advocacy added to his IEP so his teachers would be held accountable for supporting his growth and understand that it is a real challenge. I occasionally had to offer rewards to help my son overcome the anxiety of advocating for himself. He was always afraid it would make his teachers mad, and they would be upset with him for asking. In some cases, I would let the teacher know separately that he was having a lot of anxiety about asking them for help.

The idea of holding the teachers accountable and partnering with them for self-advocacy is a great idea!

Summary

1. Teach your outlier to self-advocate.

2. Break self-advocacy into detailed steps.

3. Step back into a supervisory role.

4. Intervene as needed.

5. Partner in self-advocacy.

CHAPTER 15

Being the Cheerleader

There is nobody in this world who wants our outlier to succeed more than you. You have been your child's advocate, well-wisher, and emotional support from the very beginning. You do everything to help your child be successful. For some of us, being a cheerleader may come more naturally than others. Some may be more engrossed and caught up in the day-to-day activities to get your outlier going and may not have the energy or think about cheering our outlier.

Cheering your outlier is very important for you and your outlier. It is the ongoing daily celebration of both of you and your accomplishments and the daily dose of encouragement. So, you should make cheerleading part of your daily routine. As you do this, you will get good at it! Sometimes, we must consciously remind ourselves to play this role. The daily grind may drive you to be less of a cheerleader. That's where self-care and preventing burnout, alone time, etc., that we discussed in the earlier chapters help. Alone time will give you time to reflect on how things went and what you could have done differently to improve outcomes for you and your outlier.

The word cheerleader brings to my mind the picture of a group of colorfully dressed people cheering for the players and encouraging the crowd during halftime or throughout a game. They root for individual players, the entire sports team, and the school.

Cheerleaders are characterized by hard work, positive attitude, commitment and dedication to their team, patience and persistence, confidence, and sportsmanship. Being your outlier's cheerleader is similar and includes all the same characteristics. You need a positive attitude and a strong belief that your outlier can do it! You need to exhibit the belief within yourself and express it to your outlier. You need to show your outlier in words and actions that you believe in them and that you are committed to their success. You also must show patience and perseverance.

Remember, this may not always be easy. You will need the confidence to be your outlier's cheerleader. Cheerleading should be part of the daily routine. You should cheer before and after each step forward and each milestone. Cheer when your outlier is going to try something new and is venturing out of their comfort zone.

Cheering can be as simple as saying, "I noticed you started your homework early! That's awesome. I am proud of you!" Cheering can be dramatic or silly such as, "Go {your child's name}!" It brings a smile to your outlier's face and lightens the situation. You can cheer when your outlier has tiny successes. Tell them you are very proud of them and that they will go places. Or say, "It takes a lot of courage to do what you did! I am so proud of you!" So, remember to cheer before and along the way. It is almost like saying, "I believe in you. I know you can do this!" It is also a way of saying, "Good luck! You can do this!"

You don't have to wait until the outcome or milestone is accomplished. Keep cheering along the way at each step of the journey. Once a step or goal or an intermediate result is accomplished, cheer more, reinforcing your outlier's accomplishment and showing them that you believe in them and that you are proud of your outlier. You can also mention past accomplishments when cheering for something your outlier is going to try, something that is hard or does not come easily.

For example, when your child is going to talk to the teacher about a challenge, you may cheer them on by saying, "I know it is anxiety-provoking and hard for you to talk to your teacher. I know you can do this. Remember how you met with Mrs. Pat to talk about the problem and how you resolved the issue? You can totally do this!" Once the meeting is over, and your outlier has success advocating for themselves, you may cheer, saying, "I knew you would ace this meeting! This is awesome! I am so proud of you. You are going places!" You can also simply say, "That's my boy!" or "That's my girl." Something that simple, goes a long way. My son's face always lit up whenever I said that.

So, don't forget to cheer before each step and offer encouragement and courage to your outlier. Your cheering is like soul food to your outlier. Although your outlier may not say that or acknowledge that, keep cheering. Your outlier loves the attention and energy you are exhibiting. Your outlier will always look to you for support and approval. Seeing you cheer is a sure sign of your support and approval. It gives your child the energy boost and confidence to accomplish and overcome hurdles at each step. Every change, however small, is cheer worthy.

Cheering is different from rewarding. You may throw in small rewards along the way, too. It is totally up to you to decide if something should be rewarded. Whenever your outlier overcomes something that is typically very hard, that warrants a reward. Sometimes your outlier needs cheering when they fail something. Cheering during these times is even more important than cheering when things go well. When things don't go well or seem bleak, you need to be present even more to cheer for your outlier. Tell them you believe in them and that they can do it, and that it is ok to fail.

An important aspect of being a cheerleader is showing up. If you don't show up, you will not be there to cheer your outlier. While this may be difficult if you have a full-time job or have other children and responsibilities, you must try to make this happen as much as you can. There may be situations where you cannot, which is totally ok. For example, show up to your outlier's music recital earlier. Have a little chat and cheer them on. Show up to your outlier's practice or game and cheer. Have a little chat encouraging your outlier. Show up to your Outlier's stage performance, talking before and after.

Milestones need special cheering and celebrations. When your outlier reaches special milestones, you should take time to celebrate, cheer and reward your outlier for reaching the major milestone. You should also take time to ask your outlier how they felt about reaching the milestone, what they remember about it, and what they are proud of. Talking about it will help your outlier remember and see their accomplishment. An example would be finishing an exam that was super difficult, finishing a school year, a self-advocacy outcome, etc.

While you are your child's cheerleader, you are also an important team member on your outlier's team. You may have to step up and mentor and help your child through some tasks which are challenging and need clarification of what is expected in a project or class work. You must be the lead team member, sometimes directing and driving tasks. While you should work on totally empowering your outlier, it is ok to sometimes be an active, contributing team member. Sometimes a small contribution (i.e., clarifying something, researching something, or interpreting a difficult-to-follow homework or project instruction) would go a long way in easing your outlier's anxieties and help them perform better. You would be surprised at how many schools and college instructions, and even textbooks, are written in a way that's difficult to understand. Breaking things down into smaller chunks is another way you can help your outlier.

You will always be your outlier's number one cheerleader all throughout their life. Cheerleading doesn't stop with school years. It continues well into college, graduate school, work life, and forever. How you cheer may change, but nothing else changes. The things you say may change. You will continue to be an integral part of your child's life, showing up, cheering, encouraging, being supportive, and being proud of all that your child has done and how far they have come! Keep cheering on....

Summary

1. Be your child's cheerleader.

2. Cheering versus rewarding.

3. Cheering with specific information.

4. Showing up to cheer.

5. Being on your outlier's team—being a team member who steps up to be a mentor as well as a cheerleader.

6. Keep cheering throughout your child's life.

CHAPTER 16

How To not Lose it When your Child is Losing it

I am usually pretty good at isolating my own feelings versus those of my child. I do have moments where I lose it. When I say, "lose it," I mean that my child's behavior gets the better of me and throws me off big time, leaving me sad, angry, and frustrated. This could happen anytime during your journey with your outlier. It may happen in the early stages or somewhere in the later phases of the journey—even when you are experienced in this journey.

For those of us who walk this path, this is familiar. You have a perfect day, a perfect situation, a happy moment, a cheerful day, and it's all ruined in a flash. While we are good at expecting this and mostly handle it well, there are occasions when we lose it. I want to acknowledge that this happens, and it is perfectly normal and ok for a parent to lose it occasionally when a child throws a tantrum or is losing it. We, as parents, are human, and we have feelings and emotions. We can't always be this super-parent who has it all together all the time. We have our own challenges as people. Life is not easy, in general, for most of us. We are not supernatural beings, although our job as a caretaker and parents for our outlier demands us to be close to supernatural.

The most important trait is self-empathy. When things happen, empathize with yourself, and don't be too hard on yourself that you couldn't keep it together. Being hard on ourselves makes it more difficult to rebound and fills us with guilt and anger. Remember, you have a hard job, and you made this tough choice of walking this journey with your child. So, it is ok to occasionally lose it! There may be feelings of, "Oh my God, I am not a good mother," or "Oh my God, what have I done?" or "Why couldn't I stay calm?" These feelings are perfectly normal, so don't beat yourself about them. Remember, this is a tough journey, and kindness and empathy for yourself are key to survival. Give yourself permission to lose it!

For many of us, there is no empathy from anywhere (friends or family). So, we must be our own empathizers. Take a deep breath and hug yourself and let it go. Treat yourself to a nice cup of coffee or some other treat that makes you happy. Practice calming techniques that work for you. Before you can do damage control for your outlier, taking the time to calm yourself down comes first. Note that you cannot do much of a rational job with your child when you are angry, frustrated, or upset. Going for a walk could help you calm down. Changing the immediate environment usually helps. Think of it like a timeout you give yourself to calm down. If your child is in immediate danger or needs immediate attention, then prioritize that over the task of calming down; in most situations, that will not be the case. When you are calmer, the next thing on your mind is why did this happen and how can I prevent this from happening in the future?

While we cannot mitigate and reduce every event, it is possible to avoid the frequency of such outbursts. There are no hard and fast ways to do this, but we can explore some things that work based on my experience. First and foremost, put things in perspective! What led up to the outburst? Think through the set of events that led to this point. This could give you clues about what happened and why. While doing this, you should isolate your child's behavior from yours. There are most likely different triggers for you and your child. While they are related, there may be more to your outburst than just your child's behavior.

While each situation may be quite different, some common threads are feeling like a victim, wondering or being anxious about when all this will end, feeling annoyed, drained, tired, and exhausted, Post-traumatic Stress Disorder (PTSD) is a mental health condition that's triggered by a terrifying event — (either experiencing it or witnessing it) from old situations that make you worry the behaviors are back, feeling trapped, and feeling unsupported or lonely. When you understand where you are coming from, it is easy to identify the causes and work towards fixing them. As a caregiver, you have a challenging job, and it is important for you to feel well and grounded. In my experience, most of the times I had an outburst, I was just super-tired, drained, and exhausted. This may be the most likely cause but not the only cause.

Part of you still believes and wants to see the end of this journey and for everything to be good and go well. We are human, and this is totally normal. But the reality is that there is no real end to this journey. The experiences are different and get better as you go further along, but the journey never ends. Having this perspective may help mitigate the feelings of sadness and anxiety about when this will end. Dealing with your own past experiences and any possible PTSD-like symptoms you may have by talking to a therapist could mitigate your struggles. Coming to peace with the past, if there are any shadows from the past, help as well.

Our "fight or flight" reaction may be our best-known expression of our survival instinct. This response is triggered when we (and all animals) perceive a situation as a threat to our existence; our sympathetic nervous system activates rapid emotional, psychological, and physical changes. Our outburst may be the expression of our survival instinct. There is no judgment—we just must think through the underlying causes that led us to believe this is a fight or flight situation and address why they occur.

At the end of the day, remember that you are here to influence your child and their behaviors. Suppose your child's behaviors influenced you in a way that caused you to have an outburst. In that case, it is worth pondering, thinking, and addressing the root causes. It is important to be open, humble, and grounded when you do this. There should be a neutral, troubleshooting mindset to this activity, and no judgment or bias should take place. When you work on yourself as a person, you will find yourself influencing your child in much better ways. While there is no magic bullet, here are some methods and thought processes that could help mitigate and reduce the frequency of such outbursts:

1. Put things in perspective.
2. Isolate your child's behavior from you and your love for your child.
3. Old shadows - may make you think that old behaviors are back – PTSD.
4. Victim feelings.
5. Sadness and anxiety, and whether this will ever end.
6. Feeling annoyed or drained or tired, exhausted.
7. Survival instincts.
8. Influence your child rather than your child influencing you.

Typically, outbursts also indicate some underlying problem or neglect of self-care. They may also indicate other problems and underlying issues that caused you to have an outburst. Periodically taking breaks and doing things you like or things that make you happy. For example, getting away on the weekend with a friend or going for lunch or dinner with a bestie and chatting. Taking time off for yourself is very important. You have a tough job. So, you need time off in an environment where you don't have to constantly be on your guard and be on top of things. You are human, and you need this.

Please don't feel guilty or feel that you are a bad parent when you take such breaks. You need to be your own cheerleader, cheering yourself for doing one heck of a job! Who would be courageous enough, bold enough to uptake such a task and tirelessly work on this? It is you because you are a champion! So, pat yourself on the back and give yourself credit. You should do this periodically.

Also, don't forget GRATITUDE to the Almighty on how far you have come in your journey, for all the breakthroughs, the tiny wins you have alone the away for both you and your child. Don't forget to cheer for your child and keep up the positive reinforcement. For example, you can say, "You are going to be an amazing person!", "You rock! Wow! that's my boy/girl! I was amazed at how well you handled this situation!" Make sure you are not sacrificing your self-care that we talked about in an earlier chapter. If you sacrifice self-care for longer periods of time, then such outbursts are likely to happen.

Practicing these behaviors regularly, can mitigate the frequency of times you lose it. It helps put things in perspective and see how far you have come and how far your Outlier has come in this journey. This exercise keeps you grounded. This, paired with self-care and taking breaks from your daily routine, and going to an environment that is different, will help regulate your mood. These are important, and you need to schedule them regularly to keep your sanity. Taking breaks or time off from your Outlier does not make you a bad parent.

Summary

1. Taking periodic breaks for yourself without guilt.

2. Keeping up with self-care.

3. Cheering yourself, empathizing with yourself.

4. Cheering your child, empathizing with your child.

5. Gratitude for how far you have come.

6. Gratitude for your child for how far they have come.

CHAPTER 17

When to Draw the Line as to What is Not Acceptable

While this journey has challenges along the way from younger ages to older ages, it is particularly difficult in the child's teenage years. These are the most trying years of this journey. It is a time when your outlier is going through physical and emotional changes and battling the desire to be independent while exhibiting all kinds of rebellious behaviors. While a lot of the behaviors can be attributed to the child's condition, some of them may be purely behavioral issues that will need to be addressed.

In this journey, it is hard to distinguish if a particular behavior is due to the lack of the ability of the child or is just simply rebellious bad behavior. There are cases where your child is simply being disrespectful and manipulative. I would like to hit on two key points in this section:

a. Some behaviors are unacceptable no matter what the underlying cause or reason is.

b. Not all behaviors are due to the child's condition.

While we are empathetic to our children and are always supportive of our child, there are times when you need to draw the line. This line may be different for different people based on their cultural background and upbringing, and tolerance levels. However, some things are very clear, any situation that involves physical or emotional abuse of the caregiver is a "no-no." It is simply not acceptable for the child to physically harm or emotionally abuse the parent. That's where you should draw the line!

From my own personal experience, any physical attack or physical response is unacceptable, as well as swearing or curse words. I communicated this to my outlier early on. It took a bit of time for him to understand, but it is important to stand your ground on such matters. It may be hard to reason in the moment when your outlier is having an outburst or an incident. But you should communicate ahead of time and talk to your outlier about what you won't tolerate as a parent. You can do this when your outlier is calm and relaxed or when you are going for a walk or doing something fun.

SOME BEHAVIORS ARE UNACCEPTABLE, NO MATTER WHAT THE UNDERLYING CAUSE OR REASON IS!

Let's say you have talked, communicated, and still, those behaviors came out during an outburst. You need to have ways to quickly tell your outlier that you will have no further communication, as you are hurt, and your outlier did something unacceptable. Alternatively, you can be silent. Some of us may feel that silence means disengaging with our children. You can still show presence while maintaining silence. Just being there for your child, saying absolutely nothing is being present. Some of us may not be comfortable confronting our children now of their peak outburst. Some of us may feel that it is not the child's real behavior; it is their lack of self-control making them behave like this.

My coach made the analogy of standing there and taking physical bullets shot by a child just because the child didn't mean it or did it because of their condition. Think about this! If you take the bullets, you will die or get hurt and won't be able to be there for your child. Similarly, some behaviors may leave you paralyzed or dead inside and that is why some behaviors are not acceptable, no matter what the reason or cause may be. Hence, you need to know when to draw the line. Likewise, your outlier needs to know what behaviors are unacceptable no matter what the situation or reason may be. Talking ahead of time and discussing this often may help enforce this. In my case, I had to discuss this for a while before it was fully absorbed by my outlier.

While we are good at empathizing with our children, we may often ignore signs of bad behavior, manipulation, or disrespect from our children. It is important to make that distinction. While this is not easy, it does improve with practice. Some behaviors are more obvious as bad behaviors, while others are clearly due to the lack of ability or processing power from our outlier that is causing it. Some behaviors fall in the gray area. It is hard to say if it is bad behavior or if it is due to a lack of executive function or ability. For those that are clear, you either call it out as bad behavior right away or let them go since you understand why it happened.

For those gray areas, we can apply a few rules of thumb. Ask yourself if there were alternate choices or behaviors, or reactions that were possible? If so, then you should discuss those with your child when the child calms down and reinforce those over a period.

Rehearsing or role-playing to showcase alternate responses could help. If the alternate behavior choices were not possible for your outlier because you cannot come up with the alternate behaviors naturally, then the alternate behaviors are not possible—don't overthink this. That would mean those gray areas fall under the spectrum of your child not being able to process that situation, and the gray areas need more analysis and thought. In some cases, they may remain gray. It is ok to let those go and continue your journey. If the same behaviors happen again, you can use the same analysis and actions to get more clarity and see if alternate responses are possible and discuss them with your child.

***

Summary

1. Some behaviors are unacceptable, no matter what the underlying cause or reason is.

2. Not all behaviors are due to the disability or the condition.

3. There are many gray areas.

4. Consider alternate behavior choices.

5. Rehearse or role-playing after the fact.

CHAPTER 18 –

Yes, this is Hard!

Acknowledging that this journey is hard and challenging helps put things in perspective. It also helps us not be so hard on ourselves when we lose it or when things don't go according to plan or expectations. It helps us be kind to ourselves and our outliers. Throughout this journey, you need to pause regularly to acknowledge this truth and see how far you and your child have come. While the journey has a long way to go and most likely there is no destination, celebrating successes along the way, as discussed in a previous chapter, is important. You may ask, "What do you mean by the journey has no destination?" This journey does not have one single destination. This journey is ongoing with multiple destinations and milestones.

Each time you reach one milestone/destination, there is always another destination or milestone to target. If you wait until you reach the destination (which is non-existent in reality), then you will wait for a long time. Celebrating successes along the way is like your boost for the next step. Acknowledging that this journey is hard is like your protein shake, and you need to have it often, even daily.

The other aspects of this journey are courage, creativity, and flexibility. For those of you who are reading this book and have already embarked on this journey, "KUDOS." You are courageous! You wouldn't have embarked on this journey without courage. I want to say that such a journey is not for the weak. To sustain this journey, one needs tons of courage. There will be challenges, disappointments, and frustrations along the way. You need a solid base that stems from wanting the impossible for your outlier and a willingness to do anything, even overcoming your own fears.

As Franklin D. Roosevelt said, "Courage is not the absence of fear, but the realization that something else is more important than fear itself." Wanting the success, you envision for your child more than anything else in the world will help you overcome fear and exhibit courage. Growing up, I was a timid little girl. I was an obedient, conforming child and went along with whatever happened in life. I would not have considered myself courageous. But the more I walked on this journey, the more I wanted this success for my child, and I began to overcome the fear and became courageous. I wouldn't say that there was no fear at any point in this journey. In fact, fear was and is always there in me. But realizing that I wanted this for my child more than anything helped me overcome the fear. It continues to help overcome the fear! So, if you are the fearful type, do not worry. The more you want this for your child, the more you will develop the courage to walk this journey and succeed.

Alongside courage, you will need flexibility. This is another important aspect of this journey. Things don't and won't go as planned most of the time. Many times, you must play the cards you are dealt with. You need to be a flexible thinker! In other words, you need to be able to adjust and adapt to situations in real-time. In fact, your idea of perfection or what the perfect outcome in any situation should be will also need adjustment. Another important aspect is creativity. You will need to come up with ideas on the fly. So, being creative will help. Modifying things along the way and coming up with creative solutions to your problems and your outlier's problems will be required. As you can see, this is hard but not impossible. It takes time, but it's possible!

An important part of overcoming your fears is the deep-rooted, unfailing love for your outlier. They say, "Love is God and God is love." When you have so much love for your outlier, everything falls in place. The love you have for your child will bring in the Godly strength and divine grace and become your strength. For those of us who are believers, this is called God's grace. It comes to play when you love your child. When you love your child so much, anything is possible. I always believed "God will make a way where there seems to be no way!" This firm belief and a deep love for your child will make all things possible.

Your child is a special gift from God to you. In fact, He has chosen you to be the parent of this child. This is a privilege. YES, YOU HEARD IT RIGHT! Acknowledge that you will not feel like this is a privilege as you go through the intense parts of your journey. God has chosen me to parent this child. I truly believe that and believe that if He has chosen me, He better give me the tools, skills, and whatever it takes to do this. I was often challenged in my faith as well when things got rough. But I believe that God always had my back and my outlier's back. Nonetheless, it was hard and still is!

This entire experience is very humbling. You think you know what you're doing, and then you don't. You constantly learn from your experiences. Keeping an open mind and learning from each situation is important. This entire journey is a challenge. It is a challenging game of sorts. If you think about it as a rough, hard journey, it makes it harder to go through it. Think about it like a challenging game or a puzzle and detach yourself emotionally and work through the game. Looking at it like a puzzle will make it easier—easier and not easy. This journey is never easy. You can't play this game knowing exactly what is going to happen and understanding how to handle it. Standard rules do not apply. That is why you need to keep an open mind and play your cards as they are dealt.

Being mentally ready and willing to handle anything for your outlier will be the best way to go about this journey. A deep-rooted faith to see the vision you have for your child and dream beyond what you can see will help you through this journey. As hard as this is, it is very fulfilling to see your child succeed against all odds. You may or may not have created success in the way the world sees it, but you will have given your child the outcomes and a future that was unimaginable, and this was all because you chose to tread this journey with your child. So, "HATS OFF TO YOU!"

Summary

1. Acknowledge that your journey is challenging.

2. You need courage, creativity, and flexibility.

3. You must love your child a lot, and your outlier is special and is a gift from God. God has chosen you and your outlier for a reason.

4. The entire experience is humbling and there is a lot to be learned here

5. You need real faith to see beyond what you can see

CHAPTER 19

Trusting in a Higher Power

This chapter is for those of us who believe in a higher Divine power and presence in our lives. Other readers feel free to skip this chapter. This chapter is basically to share how my own personal beliefs and faith have helped me on this journey. Each of us has our own belief systems and follows different religious practices. The core of these belief systems is that we have a higher Divine power who is always there for us and to whom we can go for help in times of need. We generally turn to this higher Divine power in difficult times. This journey with your outlier can be quite challenging at times and sometimes more difficult than others. So, turning to this Divine higher power may be needed more often for some of us. Trusting in this higher Divine power is called faith. Believing that this higher Divine power has our back always is faith. There are different ways and circumstances in which we can reach out to our faith during this journey. I will share some of these with you in this chapter.

We may ask ourselves, "Why me?" several times during this journey. Especially in times of challenges, the question will come up. This is one of the times you can tap into your faith to help answer this question. In other words, we may ask why I was chosen for this journey. Why can't I be one of the million folks who don't have to walk this journey? While there are no good explanations, our faith can help explain this. I am sharing an explanation that helped me. God has chosen you for a reason. God loves you dearly and has picked you (His angel) to take care of His child. All children, including your outlier, are God's beloved children with whom we send to this earth and put in the care of His angels. In other words, God thinks highly of you and has entrusted His child into your hands. He knows you will take good care of them. While this does not lessen any of your challenges, it does help to know that you were chosen for a reason. It gives a sense of comfort and a sense of distancing yourself from the challenges. It is almost like you are doing this for someone else who has trusted their child to you.

You are chosen—Bible verse 1 Peter 2:9 *You are a chosen generation, a royal priesthood, a holy nation, His own special people, that you may proclaim the praises of Him who called you out of darkness into His marvelous light.*

Some may struggle with, "It's all my fault!" Some of us feel a sense of guilt and feel some ownership of the struggles and challenges our child faces. This is when faith helps. Faith tells us that the child is God's child rather than your child. This disengages the ownership from you to God. So, it can't be my fault. I was chosen by God, and this child is God's child, and it is not my fault. Freedom from guilt will help direct your energies into things that matter.

There may be instances in this journey where you feel like you don't know what to do anymore, and everything is beyond you. You may reach points where you don't know what your next step should be or what you should do. In such cases, faith helps since you leave your child to God. Letting go of your child to God can help you calm down and regain a sense of normalcy. Have faith and hope and God will show you your next step.

Do not worry, but trust God— Bible verse Psalm 55:22 *Cast your burden on the Lord, and he will sustain you; he will never permit the righteous to be moved.*

Some of us in this journey are mostly alone and do not have the support of anyone else in our families. Some of us may be single parents who do not have any other support systems. In such cases, faith comes into play where you make God part of your daily journey and a partner in each step of your life. Doing so will never make you feel lonely as you know that God is always present and there for you. Knowing that you are never alone in this journey is a big relief and boosts you up and energizes you.

Many times, in this journey, you may reach a point where you do not know which way to go or what choices to make for your child, and whether you are doing the right thing. In these instances, your faith allows you to look to God for wisdom and guidance. We look to God for His wisdom, guidance, and help in making the right choice for our child. Parenting needs a lot of wisdom, boldness, and instances where you must make choices on behalf of your child. Oftentimes, this choice could be a gamechanger for your child's life and outcomes. So, it is a bit scary to be entrusted with the choices and to have to make those choices. But you can look to wisdom and guidance from God to make the right choices for your child. This will give you peace knowing that you had Divine intervention when you made a choice(s).

Ask God for direction when you don't see a way— Bible verse Jeremiah 33:3 *Call to Me, and I will answer you, and show you great and mighty things, which you do not know.*

You may reach points in your journey where you don't know what to say or don't know how to console or counsel your child. On such occasions, faith comes into play, and you just pray that God will talk to your child, counsel them, console them and talk to them. I believed on many occasions that God talked to my child and made His voice louder than all the doubts and fears that my child had and counseled my child. I truly believe and continue to believe that He has done that on several occasions and continues to do that even to this day.

Ask God for wisdom, and He will give you generously— Bible verse James 1:5 *If any of you lacks wisdom, let him ask God, who gives generously to all without reproach, and it will be given him.*

Besides all your good intentions and actions, things may not go as expected in this journey. This is another occasion where you hold on to your faith and keep going. Such situations may be discouraging and may question your ability to be on this journey. That is when you take a giant faith leap and keep going.

Also, a few times, you may have to start over. Your plans didn't have the outcomes you expected, and things didn't go well. This is never easy after investing all this time. But, sometimes, starting over or going an alternate route may be the best thing. You must try "Plan B," and you need your faith to give you the strength to start over and continue believing. You may even have to go back to the drawing board to figure out your next approach if you did not already have a Plan B. This needs a lot of strength, and that comes from God for those of us with faith.

Acknowledge that God is with you daily— Bible verse Proverbs 3:6 *In all your ways acknowledge Him, And He shall direct your paths.*

This journey, while it has its ups and downs, having a sense of gratitude and looking at all the positives can be a game changer. We must thank God each day and every moment for every little thing that went well. Every little success and change needs recognition and gratitude, and this gives enormous strength and positivity to move forward. We go about filling our days with gratitude and thanking God for everything.

Having a parent or a responsible adult who has our back no matter what gives us a sense of peace and well-being. As kids, we relied on our parents or guardians for everything, and we knew and trusted that they were there for us no matter what. Also, we could go to them and ask them what we wanted at any time. It is the same thing with our faith. We reach out to our faith and know that God is our Heavenly Father who loves us unconditionally and provides for us, protects us, and is always there for us. So, we go to Him and tell Him our needs, our wants, and the desires of our hearts. We also know that He is always with us and has our back in every situation. This frees us from all fears and doubts and gives us that childlike energy, freedom, and peace to go on with this journey.

Surrender and acknowledge it is God who is building our children— Bible verse Psalm 127:1 *Unless the Lord builds the house, those who build it labor in vain. Unless the Lord watches over the city, the watchman stays awake in vain.*

Special Inspirational Quotes from my Faith-Filled friends with children on the Autism Spectrum:

Quote 1: "Prayer was my lifeline at that time and taking part in Bible study and faith in Lord Jesus Christ."

Quote 2: "I would read about other children and progress they had made to keep my hopes up. I had my parents as support, and I prayed a lot. I was going through a particularly rough time and had a member of school administration over the Autism programs really making my son's life difficult. After a particularly tearful prayer wondering why this woman was being so awful, I received this response: "Look at what they did to my son." That puts it all in perspective."

Quote3: "Talking to other parents helped a lot. Listening to their coping methods, sometimes helping them with their issues is therapeutic as well. My trust in God sustained me a lot. Though initially I used to rant and rave at God for my plight. I learned later that there are no answers to some questions, but acceptance helps to overcome problems. There are lots of books I have read about God too, trying to make sense of the pain. But in the end, it is God I have always turned to - maybe to vent my anger and helplessness or to thank Him for the many ways He has helped me pull through. I am infinitely grateful to my family for the support system they have been and are to this day."

We can see how faith can help keep us grounded and at peace in this journey. For those of us who believe in the Divine power, let's tap into our faith and derive strength and peace for this journey.

Summary

1. Believe that you were chosen for a reason.

2. Believe that your child is God's child more than yours.

3. Leave your child to God.

4. Make God part of your daily journey and feel His presence daily every step of your way.

5. Look for wisdom and guidance when you are not sure you are making the right choice for your child.

6. In moments of despair or in cases where you don't have anything to do or say to make your child feel better, pray that God counsels them, consoles them, and talks to them.

7. Hold on to your faith when things don't go well.

8. Find the strength to start over.

9. Show gratitude for all that He has done, is doing, and is going to do.

10. Tell him what you want, knowing that he has your back.

CHAPTER 20

Living Your Life and Doing the Things You Love

While it is more time consuming initially, you will eventually be able to make time for living your life and doing the things you love to do as well while being there for your child. Once you identify what is needed and put an initial plan in place, you will have relatively more cycles to focus on things you love. You need a mindset of considering this journey as part of living and making time for other things that matter to you.

Remember you cannot wait for the end of this journey to start living your life!

Once you have a set schedule (of course we know it does not always work as planned), you can start living your life and doing the things you love to do. It won't be trivial and will need some amount of planning and creativity to follow through. We have discussed some parts of this in the self-care chapter. But you may be able to assert your needs more in the later stages of the journey than in the earlier stages. By then, hopefully your Outlier will have learned self-mastery also knows self-advocacy and is equipped to handle his/her own tasks.

You are your own person, and you have your own dreams, goals, and ambitions. While you are in this journey of caring for your children, your time and resources are limited. That does not mean that you should give up your dreams and goals completely or postpone them indefinitely. Remember there is no real end to this journey. There is only the journey and multiple intermediate destinations and no final destinations. So, it is good to acknowledge this and be creative about living this journey. By living, I mean not feeling like a victim and embracing this whole heartedly and still pursuing your dreams and goals.

Of course, such a thing is not easy. It is hard but not impossible. Hard things need creative approaches and above all a firm belief that this is possible. So, start by believing it is possible to live your life amidst all this and reach your goals and dreams. Write down where you want to go and break it down into smaller steps and see how to incrementally grow into our final full-fledged end goal. Oftentimes the goals will take multiple steps and prerequisites. Start tackling the prerequisites first. For example, if you had a goal of getting a degree or taking classes for something, break that task into steps like researching schools, researching prerequisites, costs, contacting schools, taking prerequisite classes etc. Think "PROGRESS NOT PERFECTION!".

To make time for yourself and your dreams and goals, you must make yourself a priority. You will have to believe that you totally deserve the time for yourself. Remember that not every situation warrants an emergency for your child, that you must drop all your plans and rush to it all the time. Note that there will be times like this but use your discretion. If you have set aside the time to do something for yourself, having the discipline to honor that time is important. It also helps to set up time for yourself in your schedule. Show up and do what you planned to do during that time. It also helps to have friends or accountability buddies that can come on zoom or you can meet in person and have company while you do your work. This way you are accountable and have company and motivation. You can enlist other parents or friends who are in a similar journey as buddies.

While most days things will go as planned, it is ok if you can't make it sometimes. Being harsh or beating yourself for missing something is counterproductive. Acknowledging that there may be some days where you must step out to do damage control during your me-time will allow you to handle it better and not be as disappointed. You can use the 80-20 rule where you try to make 80% of the scheduled me-time. Being creative about making time (see chapter named "Preventing burnout and thriving/being flexible") will get you closer to your own dreams. When you take the time to live your life while on this challenging journey, you feel less of a victim and feel happier and more positive. Having a growth mindset gives you a higher chance of succeeding in your own goals and dreams. Flexibility and creativity are equally important in making this work like making time for self-care. In fact, making time for your future dreams and goals is a form of self-care.

According to a google search:

"Growth mindset describes a way of viewing challenges and setbacks. People who have a growth mindset believe that even if they struggle with certain skills, their abilities aren't set in stone. They think that with work, their skills can improve over time."

Always keep this in mind and remind yourself that progress is more important than perfection or a rapid completion of your goals. This approach will make sure you reach your goals and dreams although it may seem slower initially but slowly and surely you will accomplish what you meant to be. Remember there are many paths to reach a place.

You can totally follow your dreams and make them a reality too!

Summary

1. Acknowledging that the journey has no destination

2. Learning to live in this journey and not feel like a victim

3. Starting small and growing your dreams

4. Making yourself a priority (not every situation warrants an emergency for your child)

5. Being regular no matter what and have accountability buddies if possible

6. There may be some days you must come back and do damage control and that is ok

7. Being creative to making time for your long-term dream

CHAPTER 21

Caring for Your Other Children

As a parent raising your little outlier, much of your bandwidth goes into caring for your Outlier. If you have other children, obviously this affects the time you can give to them. I decided to add this chapter to acknowledge this and share some ways of how you can spend time with your other children as well.

My other child had to grow up fast, mature quickly, and handle things mostly on her own much earlier. While working a full-time job, being a homemaker, and caring for a child who had different needs, there was not a whole lot of time or energy that I had to spend with my other child. Just doing the basic care and a few chats and hugs here and there is all I could do for my her. In the early days, I didn't realize that this was happening. I would like to share that being mindful that this could happen to your other children early on would help a lot. When you don't even realize that this is happening, then it is not possible to find creative ways to solve this.

I was too caught up in the daily tasks and the numerous "to-dos." My other child had no choice but to take care of herself most of the time. She was also more mature for her age and understood the situation well at a young age. She wanted to help me whenever possible. She took the task of handling things on her own so she wouldn't add to my workload. She is a sweet angel and God's gift to me. I won't say I spent a lot of time with her, but the times we spent were the most memorable ones, which we fondly recall even to this day.

After a few years, when my other child had some outbursts on certain occasions, I realized that I had not spent enough time with her. When I realized this, I felt terrible. It was not my intention. I did not recognize when this was happening. Once I realized she needed more time with me, I made it a priority. After that, I was always intentional and mindful of the needs of my daughter too. While carving out this kind of time was not easy, it is totally possible with some creativity and intention. Note that the amount of time you have for your other child will be limited, and hence, it is important to make that time count. In other words, make it quality time. Be very intentional about the time you spend with your other child.

Start off with an honest conversation with your other child and be straightforward and explain your situation. Being honest about what is going on and your time constraints will really help. When I was honest, my other child was very supportive and even stepped up to help me in several situations. It also sets realistic expectations. To this day, we have such good conversations, and we are best friends.

Once you are intentional and make it a priority, you can start off with daily check-ins. Talk to your other child one-on-one daily, checking in about how their day went and some of the highlights. This is to tune into what is happening in the other child's life. Ask about their day, friends, and little things that happened. When you are doing this, make sure you are doing this with 100% of your attention with no distractions. This time should be fully dedicated to your other child, even if it means saying no to your Outlier or other priorities. This time does not have to be too long, but long enough to chat and connect with your other child. Make sure you do this daily and make it part of your routine.

Make appreciation part of that conversation or interaction. Again, be intentional about this. Make sure you recognize your other child's actions that help you and your Outlier. Let the other child know how special they are, and how much you appreciate them. Call out specifics and thank the child and praise the child. The things you are appreciating or thanking your other child do not need to be major. You can say something like, "Thank you for being patient and waiting your turn, thank you for helping pack the lunches this morning, thank you for being ready earlier," or "You did a great job helping empty the dishwasher—it really helped me in not feeling overwhelmed," or "You are my God sent angel, what would I do without you," or simply "I love you!"

Carve out short times throughout the week for your other child. For example, you can take your other child on your walk and chat and laugh together. You can also talk to your other child alone on your errands. This will give you time to bond one-on-one. You can also drive together to get ice cream or to the bookstore or library. A lot of chatting can go on during the drive. My daughter was an early riser, and we had chats during weekend morning breakfasts, or we would drive to the farmer's market together, chatting, laughing, and sharing our stories.

I would make special chocolate chip pancakes for her on weekend mornings, and this was something she cherishes even now. We do that whenever she visits from college, and it has become a fond memory. Also, I would take off early from work some days to go watch her home games. I would be there to cheer her on. This was also very special to my daughter. I would make it to most home games.

Periodically, go away on short weekend trips or do special things with your other child. This can be done every few months. In my case, my other child played volleyball which had weekend games that were usually a one to two hours' drive from our home. I would drive her to the away games. The ride gave us a lot of time to chat, bond, and spend time together. Also, being at the game and cheering for her was part of my intentional time spending with her.

I have also volunteered to be the team mom for the tournaments in other states. This gave us a lot of time to be together. These are very special memories that we both cherish to this day. One of our fond memories is getting food from Panda Express in an away town after a long day's game and watching the show "Modern Family" together. It was a funny memory as we both craved Panda Express food during that trip and drove quite a bit to find a Panda Express after a long day of games.

As I end this chapter, I wanted to share something I found years ago in the form of a video that someone shared. For a long time, I did not have a good answer to the question asked by my other child.

The question was, "Why do I not get rewarded like my brother for even small things he does while I just get a "good job" when I do good things, and I'm a good person every day?" I always wondered what the right answer might be. Then someone shared this video, which was about a reply to a child's question given by a writer of the "Kids News" column in the *Chicago Tribune*. His name was Mr. Kuester. You can Google and read about him and this story. One of the kids wrote him a letter asking why her mother only praised her for a good job when she did something right and did not reward her like she rewarded her brother for even small things he did.

The writer's response was: "Making you a good child is God's highest reward to you." I forwarded the video to my daughter; I think that was a very good answer to the question. This does not mean that your outlier is not a good child, but you get the idea.

Summary

1. Most kids are understanding - be honest and share your outlier's situation with the other child. They will understand and, in fact, may even help you.

2. Be very intentional about the time you spend with your other children.

3. Have daily check-in with the other children.

4. Tell them how special they are.

5. Carve out short times throughout the week and make that time count.

6. Go away on trips or do special things with that child periodically.

CHAPTER 22

Conclusion

No matter what you hear from other people, you are the one who knows your child the best. You have the ability, resources, and tools to help your child find a path forward to success. You have the ability and power to troubleshoot, create a vision for your neuro-divergent child, put a plan in place and execute it. You will see positive outcomes for you and your child. You are the best parent, mentor, and cheerleader your child can ever have. Continue to support your child as you see fit and don't forget to celebrate yourself and your child at each step. Remember always that you are closest to your child and know the best course of action in every situation. You only must only really want that vision for your child, believe and work towards it.

You will continue to be your child's cheerleader throughout this journey as you witness the great things your child will accomplish. Even as your child gets older and becomes more independent, they will always be your special child and will have a special place in your heart. With your unfailing love and perseverance, you can and will see authentic success for your child. KEEP CHEERING ON!

ABOUT THE AUTHOR

As a mother to a son on the Autism spectrum, I have a first-hand experience of living the journey of raising an Outlier. Through faith and perseverance, a success story has emerged from this journey. Today my son is an independent confident young man with a master's degree and a good job. He is on route to writing more amazing success stories of his own. It was great to share my journey with you all. I have chosen to publish my book on a pen name to protect the privacy of my family. While all people in this story are real, the names of my friends have also been changed to protect their privacy. Please share your feedback and thoughts on my website: www.mylittleoutlier.com.

I would be happy to talk to each of you who are going through similar journeys and share my own experiences from my journey. Please share your thoughts on the book and contact me at mylittle-outlier@gmail.com to brainstorm ideas for situations in your own journey or if you just want to chat, talk through ideas, or just be heard.